Alan Jacobs has made a lifelong study of mysticism and is a regularly published author and poet. He is the editor of *Poetry for the Spirit, Tales from Rumi, Native American Wisdom* and the beautiful poetic translations of *The Upanishads* and *The Gnostic Gospels,* later expanded into *The Essential Gnostic Gospels.* He lives in London.

WHEN JESUS LIVED IN INDIA

The Quest for the Aquarian Gospel:
the Mystery of the Missing Years

Alan Jacobs

WATKINS PUBLISHING
LONDON

Distributed in the USA and Canada by Sterling Publishing Co., Inc.
387 Park Avenue South, New York, NY 10016

Text Copyright © Alan Jacobs 2009

Designed and typeset by Jerry Goldie

Printed in the U.S.A.

ISBN-13: 978-1-906787-29-5

Contents

Acknowledgements

To Michael Mann for encouraging me to write this book.
To the staff of The British Library for greatly assisting my
research.

The author and publisher wish to thank all those copyright
holders, too numerous to mention, who have given permission
for an extract of their work to appear. If, however, there are
any omissions we will be pleased to correct the matter in any
future editions.

'History is only legend that is agreed upon.'

Anon

'The value of myth is not in its truth as fact, but in its truth as meaning.'

Michael Horan

'We have to learn to let God show us what he wants us to see.'

Karl Barth

'Wise Men came from the East to the cradle of the infant Christ. Is it not time that we paid them a return visit?'

Dean Inge

'And there are also many other things which Jesus did, which, if they should be written every one, I suppose that even the world itself could not contain the books that should be written.'

John Chapter 21 verse 25

Introduction

When *Jesus Lived in India*. At first sight such an extraordinary title seems a bizarre fantasy, a preposterous historical impossibility, some exotic romantic dream! However, surprising as it may seem, this is not at all the case, and it is far from being an eccentric, fanciful speculation. This legend has been generally accepted in Tibet, Nepal, northern India and Kashmir for over 2,000 years. There, not only do scriptural and archaeological evidence exist, but the legend is so firmly rooted in popular folk memory that it is regarded as a certainty. Of course, in the Western Christian world such an idea has been disregarded, and even condemned, as it totally contradicts the accepted scriptural life and crucifixion of Jesus.

Yet this startling idea has been circulating since the 19th century amongst academic and biblical scholars in Europe, America and India, and is soon to confront the world in the form of a film which portrays Jesus' life and mission in India, Tibet, Nepal and elsewhere.

The American and Indian film industries have at last joined together to make a religious epic entitled *The Aquarian Gospel*. It fills in the 'missing years' of Jesus in India, Tibet, Nepal, Kashmir and elsewhere, from the ages of 12 to 30, when 'the boy grew in stature and wisdom' as it is written in the New Testament gospels. The film is expected to arouse the same interest and debate as the famed *Da Vinci Code*. It is based on The Aquarian Gospel and Holger Kersten's book *Jesus Lived in India*. Both of these works I will be discussing fully.

This will not be the first film to cover this fascinating subject. Movie director Paul Davids has made a film entitled *Jesus in India* which tackles the provocative task of separating myth and legend from historical evidence. In this film, an adventurer called Edward Martin determines to visit the Hemis Monastery to find the Missing Gospel of Issa. There is much discussion in the film, for and against the hypothesis, by various experts including the Dalai Lama, biblical scholar Elaine Pagels, Muslim scholar Arif Khan, and Monsignor Corrado Balducci, Apostolic Nuncio of Pope John Paul II. In addition to these two films, Indian producer Subhrajit Mitra has made a movie entitled *The Unknown Stories of the Messiah*, which covers the same ground as Holger Kersten's book *Jesus Lived in India*. A documentary film was also made by Richard Bock in 1975, called *The Lost Years of Jesus*, in which he followed Nicolai Notovitch's journey through India and Tibet. The film includes an introduction from Professor John C Trever of the Claremont School of Theology, and the actor William Marshall reads from the Gospel of Issa. Janet Bock has written an accompanying book called *The Jesus Mystery*. There is also an entertaining novel called *The Rozabel Line* by the Indian writer Ashwin Sanghi, published in 2007. This is a murder mystery but manages to incorporate most of the story of Jesus in India in its pages. The Bibliography lists many of the growing number of books relevant to this whole controversial question.

It is the purpose of this book to take a long, hard look at the whole question of whether Jesus did or did not visit India and

Tibet. I shall present impartially all the evidence for and against such a supposition, which I gathered after lengthy research, so that the reader can form his own reasoned judgement on this tantalizing theory which has stimulated filmmakers, authors and biblical scholars, both in the East and West, for over a century.

Astonishingly, no details are given by the Four Evangelists as to where Jesus went and what he did to 'increase in stature' during these entire 19 years! It is one of the great biblical and historical mysteries. Many theories exist about how Jesus could have spent his adolescence and entry into manhood, and I shall examine the most important of them, as well as the Indian and Tibetan legends, as our book proceeds. Islamic scholars have a great deal to say on this topic which I shall also review.

However, the modern, apocryphal Aquarian Gospel, rather than the ancient canonical gospels, tells us in precise detail all about Christ's mission to India, Tibet and Nepal, and his adventures there. The actual historical and archaeological evidence that Jesus may have indeed spent his 'missing years' in Tibet, Nepal and Kashmir, was first brought to light in the late-19th century by the then famous Russian author and explorer, Nicolai Notovitch. It is on Notovitch's discoveries, along with the Aquarian Gospel, that the latest motion picture has been based.

This legend first caught my imagination when I was last in India. I read about the proposed film and I was inspired to write and research a book which would impartially investigate all the evidence, so as to leave the inquisitive reader in a position to decide the truth or falsehood of such an idea. My research has been a fascinating journey of discovery, which I have endeavoured to convey in a straightforward manner. I include many references from the considerable literature which has appeared on this enthralling subject. It has been for me, more in the nature of an investigative detective story, rather than a scholastic examination.

It is essential in this present era when humanity's religious faith is being undermined by sceptics and atheists in the name of science, that the real facts about Jesus' actual life are brought closer to the light, so that we can begin to separate myth and legend from history. Although one book cannot solve this great problem conclusively, it raises the discussion to a level where the interested reader will find enough information to make reasonable judgements for him- or herself.

Myths and legends are extremely powerful, and often portray a profound truth which is meaningful to millions of men and women who inherit a tradition of events from the ancient past. It would be a pity if myth and legend, so dependent on the collective folk memory, were completely destroyed by a rigid pedantry which insists that everything is either supported by archaeological and documentary records, or else firmly dismissed out of hand.

Alan Jacobs
London, September 2008

Chapter 1

The Evidence of Levi Dowling, Nicolai Notovitch and Holger Kersten

*The Brahmanic Masters wondered at the clear
conception of the child, and often were amazed when
he explained to them the meaning of the laws.*

The Aquarian Gospel, chapter 22 verse 20

W e now enjoy living in the roseate dawn of the Age of
Aquarius, the Water Bearer, the Truth Bearer. According
to the astrological naming of time periods, which change about
every 2,000 years, we have left the Piscean Age when the original
gospels of Jesus Christ's great mission on Earth were first given,
and we have now entered a new era, when a new gospel has
been revealed, appropriate to our Aquarian Age.

The Piscean Age is identical with the first Christian
Revelation. Pisces means fish. This is a water sign, water symbol-
izing truth. In the early days of the Christian era, the fish was an
emblem of the faith, which appeared inscribed on the catacombs
of the persecuted Christians, hiding from Roman wrath under
the insane Emperor Nero, who made the allegation that they
had tried to burn down the capital. But, the Aquarian Age is

pre-eminently a spiritual age, strongly reacting against contemporary materialism. The deeper, more esoteric teachings of Jesus are more suitable to the modern world, and according to their believers are given through the revelation of this new Aquarian Gospel.

The Gospel contains 22 sections, divided into separate chapters, on Jesus' life and works, and covers over 260 pages. There have been 53 reprints of the book since it first appeared in 1908, and it continues to be reissued. In this book we shall necessarily concentrate on the chapters actually referring to Jesus' time in India and Tibet, during his 'missing years', although the text covers his journey through ancient Greece, Persia and other regions on his route. However, India and Tibet are the dedicated subjects of our quest for investigating the truth of the Aquarian Gospel, and our wish to discover whether or not Jesus ever really visited these far-off lands. The relevant information is contained in chapters V, VI, VII, and XXI of the Gospel.

In the 20th and 21st centuries of the new Aquarian Age, many dramatic changes have already become apparent. Alternative medicine, astrology, vegetarianism, ecology, electronic communications and the literature of Western and Eastern mysticism are all gaining in popularity with millions, both in the East and West, in a way that is unprecedented in previous times. It can indeed be called a New Age. The Aquarian Gospel, necessarily suited to this radically different, historical period, was revealed to the highly gifted spiritual and psychic medium, the Reverend Dr Levi H Dowling (1844–1911). Born into a devoutly religious family, his father was a minister of the respected North-Western, American Christian Denomination, the Disciples of Christ. Following in his father's footsteps, Levi was a prodigious child preacher, and began to enthuse large congregations from the early age of 16. As a young man he served in the United States Army as a chaplain, during the American Civil War. He attended the North-Western Christian University at Indianapolis, and graduated from two medical colleges before practising medicine until retirement, when he also began his serious literary work.

According to his biographer (and second wife), Dr Eva S Dowling, 'after forty years of profound study and silent meditation, he entered deeply into the study of ethereal or heavenly vibrations. He found himself miraculously placed into that higher state of spiritual consciousness which allowed him to enter the world of those superfine ethers called the "Akashic".' The 'Akashic' may be defined simply as the Kingdom of Supreme Intelligence, or Universal Mind. Akasha is Sanskrit for sky, space or ether, and these records denote a vast collection of encoded knowledge, stored in a non-physical plane of existence. They record every event in the history of the cosmos, impressed on the somniferous ether or Akasha. It was from this realm that Dowling became 'The Chosen Channel', and received his New Gospel of Christ Jesus for the Aquarian Age. This revelation has influenced many Christian sects allied to the extensive Disciples of Christ movement in America, such as the Aquarian Christine Church Universal, the Saint Germain Foundation and the Church Universal Triumphant. The book has also enjoyed a much wider readership, East and West, among those interested in refined spiritual literature, and the many growing adherents of the New Age movement.

Levi Dowling was born in 1844 and was regarded at the time as an extraordinary child prodigy, commencing his pastoral ministry at the age of 16. He also successfully practised medicine in Ohio until his death in 1911. No exact date is given for the completion of his Aquarian Gospel, but in her introduction to his book, Dr Eva Dowling gives us Levi's own account of how he received the Aquarian Gospel. I have extracted the important verses appertaining to our quest, that Dowling wrote in his own introductory poem entitled 'The Cusp of the Ages'.

> In Spirit I was caught away into the realms of Akasha;
>   I stood alone within the circle of the Sun.
>
> And there I found the secret spring that opens up the
>   door to Wisdom and an understanding heart.
>
> I entered in and then I knew ...
>
> And then I stood upon the cusp where Ages meet.
>   The Piscean Age had passed; the Aquarian Age
>   had just begun.
>
> And then I heard the Aquarian Cherubim and
>   Seraphim proclaim the Gospel of the coming Age,
>   the age of Wisdom, of the Son of Man.
>
> This Gospel I will tell, and I will sing this song in every
>   land, to all the people, tribes and tongues of earth.

Consequentially, the Aquarian Gospel presented a new and completely radical vision of the mission and teachings of Jesus Christ, which its many adherents consider to be more relevant and applicable to our troubled times than the synoptic gospels. As this fascinating tale develops we shall follow all the supporting evidence for Dowling's assertion that Jesus visited India in the 'missing years'. It is an exciting series of events, with all the twists, and turns of a mystery story. This is our quest for the Aquarian Gospel which we will examine in more detail in our next chapter.

The legend that Jesus of Nazareth spent his 'missing years' in India first surfaced in the West at the end of the 19th century with a sensational bestseller written by the remarkable Russian scholar, soldier, explorer, journalist, author and historian, Nicolai Notovitch. He published his book in Paris, which became widely read in the 1890s, entitled *La Vie Inconnue de Jesus Christ*. This was first translated into English by Violet Crispe in 1895, and published in London. There were several other editions translated into all the major European languages. I found this rare book, in a slightly battered condition, in the archives of the British Library and studied it extensively, along with all the other significant literature that I could find. Notovitch's book caused a great sensation at the time, because in his exploratory travels in India and Tibet, he was convinced that he had discovered certain documentary evidence that proved, beyond any doubt, that Jesus Christ definitely lived in India and visited Tibet during his so-called 'missing years'.

There has been endless speculation about these missing, hidden, secret or lost years, as they are variously called. The New Testament is inexplicably silent about how and where Jesus lived in the time from when he discoursed with the elders in the Temple, at the age of 12, until he reappeared in Jerusalem to commence his great, historic mission at the age of 30. The main references are in Luke's gospel, chapter 2, from verse 42 onwards. 'When he was 12 years old, they [the holy family], went up to Jerusalem after the custom of the feast ... as they returned the child Jesus tarried behind in Jerusalem and Joseph and his mother knew not of it ... After three days they found him in the temple, sitting in the midst of the doctors, both hearing them and asking them questions ... And he went down with them [the Holy Family] and came to Nazareth ... And Jesus increased in wisdom and stature and in favour with God and man.' He then only reappears to be baptized by John the Baptist in Luke, chapter 3 verse 23: 'And Jesus himself began to be about thirty years of age ...' He commences his ministry in chapter 4 when he sojourns in the wilderness and is tempted by the Devil. Then the gospel story continues until the Resurrection. The other gospels are also inexplicably silent, so we are left with a great mystery, about which there has been endless speculation.

One theory is that he spent his time in Jerusalem, simply working in his father's carpentry workshop. More plausibly there is a suggestion that he disappeared into either an Essene or Theraputae community, for further spiritual preparation, before he was ready to embark on his great mission. Then there is the other theory that he travelled to distant lands. It is this supposition that prompted the author and explorer Nicolai Notovitch to commence his search in Asia and the Far East for evidence. He was convinced he had solved the great riddle, and his book *The Unknown Life of Jesus* stunned his contemporaries, with the startling revelation that Jesus had actually journeyed to India and Tibet during those mysterious missing 19 years.

The Koran has many verses concerning Jesus, and Islamic scholars, principally Dr Hadhrat Mirza Ghulam Ahman of Qadian, Abdul Aziz Kashmiri, and the Sufi Professor Dr Fida Hassnain all believe, based on Koranic verses, that Jesus escaped the crucifixion, then travelled to Kashmir where he lived and died. I shall review this strongly held Islamic point of view in chapter 9.

This discovery by Notovitch was compounded by the

astonishing revelation of 'The Aquarian Gospel', which I discussed in the Introduction, and would seem to confirm the discoveries which the explorer Notovitch believed to be true, although the narrative and details do not exactly correspond. Whether Levi Dowling ever read Nicolai Notovitch's book, or whether Nicolai Notovitch ever read the Aquarian Gospel, we shall never know.

Nicolai Alexandrovitch Notovitch, born in 1858, was a prolific Russian author and historian. In 1887 he made a journey to India as the Far Eastern correspondent of the quality Russian Journal *Novaya Vremiya*, with the express purpose of sending articles of interest found on his travels in Asia. He travelled as far as Kashmir, then on to the hidden city of Ladakh, in Tibet. There in Ladakh, he chanced to visit a Buddhist monastery, where in conversation with the head lama, he was informed of their belief that the spirit of Buddhist teachings was actually enshrined in the teachings of Christianity, through the visit of the prophet Issa to Tibet approximately 2,000 years ago. Astonishingly, the lama's description of Issa seemed, to Notovitch, to conform with the personage of Jesus Christ, and he determined then and there fully to investigate the truth of this legend. The lama directed him to the monastery of Hemis, near Leh, in Ladakh, where he would find the documentary evidence. There, following enquiries with the abbot of Hemis, he requested to see any manuscripts relating to the prophet Issa's visit to Tibet. The abbot kindly obliged, by reading certain single verses, with the aid of a translator, from an ancient manuscript. This narrative Notovitch recorded and summarized. I will relate this gospel from his rendition, in chapter 3.

A brief introduction describes the early history of the Israelites and the life of Moses. An account follows of how the

Holy Spirit periodically assumes human form so He may demonstrate the Divine Wisdom for mankind in practice. One of these avatars or messengers of God was born in Judea and given the name of Issa, which is significantly close to Isa, the Muslim name for Jesus. Sometime around the age of 14 the youth arrived in the region of the Indus, in the company of merchants, following the ancient Silk Route, where he settled among the Aryans with the intention of furthering his self-perfection, and studying the revelations of the Hindu sages, in particular that of the Buddha, born over 500 years before Issa himself. The young Issa travelled in the Punjab, visited the Jains, and met the Brahmans of Jagannath, where he studied the Vedas. He eventually left India having displeased the Brahmans by his castigation of the caste system, which took away from the lower castes their fundamental human rights as children of God, their heavenly Father. Issa travels on to Nepal, where he studies the Buddhist Scriptures, before returning to his own people who were suffering severe affliction at the hands of Imperial Rome. There in Jerusalem he commences his great, historic mission on Earth, as the New Testament records. According to Notovitch all the passages which were translated to him were collections of ancient Tibetan writings, in the Pali language, and compiled around 200 years after the birth of Christ, and preserved in a monastery in Lhasa near the Potala Palace, home of the Dalai Llama.

On his return to Russia Notovitch succeeded in having his sensational manuscript published in Paris rather than Moscow, as the Russian authorities believed it to be subversive in its undermining of the doctrine of the Russian Orthodox Church. It was therefore written in French and published with the title

La Vie Inconnue de Jesus Christ. It was translated into English in 1895. The book caused a sensation both amongst the international public and the Christian authorities, and scholars and historians. Professor Dr Max Muller, the celebrated Oxford professor, and editor of the 50-volume *Sacred Books of the East* was a convinced Christian, and was said to be very unhappy with such a discovery. He sent a school teacher from the Government College in Agra, one Archibald Douglas, on to Tibet in order to verify Notovitch's claims. Although Douglas never succeeded in examining the manuscripts he nevertheless partisanly denied their existence. However, 40 years before Notovitch's visit to Hemis, according to the German academic and religious historian Dr Holger Kersten, author of the book *Jesus in India*, a lady by the name of Mrs Harvey, in a book entitled *The Adventures of a Lady in Tartary, Thibet, China and Kashmir*, published in 1853, describes the Tibetan manuscripts, which were later read to Notovitch. After Notovitch, Kaliprasad Chandra of the Oriental Seminary in Calcutta visited Tibet. He went to Hemis where the monks reported Notovitch's report to be truthful, and he was shown the manuscripts. This account was published in his book *Kashmir and Tibet*. In 1925, the Russian archaeologist Nicholas Roerich, who spent most of his life in India, made reference in his writings to the Tibetan documents in Ladakh, whereby it was stated that 'Jesus had returned from the Himalaya to Palestine at the age of twenty-nine'. In 1931 Lady Henrietta Merrick's book *In The World Attick* allegedly contained the statement: 'In Leh is the legend of Christ who is called "Issa" where the monastery at Hemis holds precious documents 1,500 years old which tell of the days that he passed in Leh, where he was joyously received and where he preached.' In 1939 the Swiss nun, the Revd. Mother Elizabeth Caspari visited Hemis Monastery in the company of Mrs Clarence Gasque, the esteemed President of the World Association of Faith, when the librarian showed them the original ancient manuscripts that were read to Notovitch. Dr Holger Kersten, however, who also visited Tibet, found that the texts have since been moved to an unknown destination. We shall return with a full examination of Nicolai's discoveries in our concluding chapter, but first we need to examine the writings of Dr Holger Kersten.

Dr Holger Kersten is a respected academic author and scholar, specializing in religious history. He studied theology and pedagogy at the University of Freiberg, and has travelled extensively in the Middle East and India. He is the author of the much discussed, best-selling *Jesus Lived in India*. This book has since been translated into 15 different languages, and has gained worldwide attention. It is still in print by Penguin Books. Kersten visited India in 1979, and in Dharamsala he requested a letter of introduction from the Tibetan authorities to the abbot of the Hemis monastery in order to inspect the manuscripts about which Nicolai Notovitch had written. Kersten received the necessary document, and eventually arrived at Hemis. While waiting for his audience he learned that the former abbot of Hemis had been reported missing since the invasion of Tibet by Chinese Communist troops. The Chinese Government had prohibited all correspondence with him, and the last anyone had heard of the Hemis high lama was that he was held as a prisoner in a labour camp. After 15 years, he was assumed to have died and a successor was found. When Kersten was summoned for his audience with the new high lama, he was accompanied by an interpreter. He showed the abbot his letter of introduction and told him how very important these texts would be for the whole of Christendom. The venerable abbot informed him that the scriptures in question had already been searched for, but nothing could now be found. He left feeling very disappointed, but later managed to discover that an old diary dating from the 19th century was located in the Moravian Church Mission in Leh, in which the missionary and Tibetan scholar Dr Karl Marx (not to be confused with the author of *Das Kapital*) had mentioned Notovitch's stay at the Hemis monastery. He visited the Moravian Mission but Father Razu, the director, could not show him the precious diary because it had mysteriously disappeared three years earlier. The friendly priest had no explanation for the book's disappearance but recalled that a certain Professor, Dr Fida Hassnain from Srinigar had taken photographs of the relevant pages, and had supplied the German *Stern* magazine with the report, and a photograph was published in 1973.

Thus Dr Kersten was satisfied that Notovitch had actually visited the monastery as he claimed. He then went to Kashmir and visited the venerable and distinguished Islamic, Sufi scholar Professor Fida Hassnain at the University of Kashmir. He agreed to inform Kersten all about his research into this question. But Kersten found that in his opinion, his evidence was mainly by implication, association and apparent connections, rather than based on solid scientific facts. Kersten determined that the professor's research had to be placed on a firm scientific footing. This resulted in Kersten's own book *Jesus Lived in India*. He felt certain that a story so highly respected by revered Tibetans, and maintained for over 2,000 years, must have some foundation in folk memory, although difficult to prove. Folk memory and legend invariably free us from the difficult weight of impossible scientific exactitude. Nevertheless these legends strongly resonate with those who hear of them, as somewhere the likelihood of their truth seems to lie in humanity's archetypal, collective memory.

Kersten knew that Issa was somewhat similar to the name commonly used for Jesus in Kashmir, Yuz Azaf; and most likely to Isa, as used in Islam. Isa or Issa derives from the Syriac Yeshu, which comes from Jesus' name in Aramaic, Yeshua or Joshua, the son of Joseph. Jesus is the Greek form, and Christos means Saviour. *Jesus in India*, by the Islamic scholar Hadhrat Mirza Ghulam Ahmad of Qadian, born in 1835, strongly supports the theory that Issa, known in Tibet and Kashmir, was in fact Jesus of Nazareth. I shall refer to this scholarly and respected book wherever appropriate in chapter 7 on the Islamic point of view. In Islam, Jesus is thought of as the last great prophet before Muhammad. Ahmad states that the Koran confirms the truth that Jesus was saved from a death that would have been unworthy of him, then travelled with merchants to India and stayed in Kashmir until his death, where he was buried in a tomb which still exists. I shall quote the relevant verses from the Koran in chapter 7. This led Kersten to follow further trails fully outlined in his book. One was to point out the many similarities in Christ's preaching with the Buddha's teaching, particularly in the Beatitudes. He also followed up the legend in Kashmir that Issa was buried there, having escaped the crucifixion. He visited the tomb, which I shall also discuss in chapter 7. Kersten also discovered that amongst the ancient sacred Hindu texts, the Puranas, there existed the Bhavishyat Maha Purana and the Natha Namavali Sutra, written between the 3rd and 7th centuries AD and containing significant supplements that describe how Jesus came to India. I shall transcribe these verses in chapter 6.

Kersten maintains that there is further evidence for the presence of Jesus in Kashmir which is much more solid than mere oral and even the Puranic tradition. There is a tomb of the prophet Yuz Asaf (Kashmiri term for Jesus) located in Srinigar. Above the entrance to the burial chamber is carved an inscription which declares that Yuz Asaf entered Kashmir many centuries ago. This would tally with the Koran, whereby Jesus escaped death from the crucifixion. The tomb points to his actual death, much later, in Kashmir. Kersten also refers to other references in Hindu texts to Jesus having visited Kashmir. Dr Kersten's research is long, scholarly and exhaustive. It is necessary to study his book for his entire thesis, of which this is a brief summary. 'The Aquarian Gospel' revealed by Dr Levi H Dowling is quite adamant that Jesus visited India and Tibet. Dr Dowling devotes three chapters to his stay in India and Tibet which I shall fully render in chapter 2. In the final chapter, I shall discuss Notovitch, Kersten and Dowling's claims, as well as the several contrary opinions, so that the reader may form his or her own judgement on their veracity.

Chapter 2

From The Aquarian Gospel: Jesus in India and Tibet

The Aquarian Gospel of Jesus the Christ, has had a very considerable influence amongst Christian mystical sects, and the worldwide New Age movement. The book has run into innumerable editions and has never been out of print since the charismatic Levi Dowling revealed it to the world as a direct transmission from the Kingdom of Supreme Intelligence. As a mere youth, Dowling had a vision in which he was told that he was to 'build a white city'. This vision was repeated three times in his later years. Dowling believed that the 'white city' was the Aquarian Gospel transmitted to him over a period of time in the small hours of the morning. None of this lessens the charm or the esoteric insight of this book. Nor should its subterranean impact on popular spirituality in the United States be underestimated. The Aquarian Gospel was rediscovered during the spiritual ferment of the 1960s; a copy of this book was almost *de rigueur* in many New Age households, and it no doubt played an unsung role in naming this era as the 'Age of Aquarius'. Although they might never admit it, many a staid evangelical Christian probably had their spiritual awakening while coming under its influence.

This 260-page gospel covers a very wide field. It has 22 sections each containing a different number of chapters. It is written in what may be described as neo-biblical language, echoing much of the cadence contained in the New Testament. It commences with the Annunciation and Jesus' early life and education, and then jumps to the 'missing years' when we find Jesus travels to India, Tibet and then western India. He returns through Persia, Assyria, Greece and Egypt, back to Jerusalem. It tells about the ministry of John the Baptist whom it calls the 'Harbinger', and then Jesus' own ministry, ending with his betrayal, trial, execution, and resurrection and the establishment of the Christian Church. It is full of startling esoteric ideas which have inspired fringe sects and cults to a mystical interpretation of Jesus' teaching not encountered since the early apocryphal Gnostic gospels in the mediaeval world. It has received a great deal of attention both by enthusiasts and critics.

The author Michael F O'Keefe has written this enthusiastic commendatory review, in the public domain, which illustrates how sincere devotees of the Aquarian Gospel feel about the book.

> In this marvellous book of Christ, Jesus reveals that every living thing is a deity manifest, and each has a soul, which is on a very long trek – from total unawareness of its own divinity, to full consciousness. Every creature, after many incarnations, eventually becomes fully aware of its own divine lineage; and later, during subsequent incarnations, each one learns more and more about developing and exercising divine Strength, Wisdom and Love; until eventually, every one (plant, animal and human) achieves pure perfection –

oneness with God (our Father). He said that he, Jesus, is our example of a man who achieved oneness. He also proclaimed that he is simply our elder brother, come to teach us; and that he is our example of that which we all will eventually become. Jesus, the first person of Earth's history to conquer death, said, 'You may follow me,' and thus, he leads the way. He became immortal. He is always with us. He and those who followed him continually labor for us (beyond the veil), so that we too may learn, and become wise and strong enough to follow him. As they constantly labor for us, they also patiently wait for us. The Book of God's Remembrance is a recording – imprinted on disc-like plates smaller than atoms. Every event that ever occurs leaves an imprint on these elemental particles, which continuously emit extremely fine energy waves. Anyone who knows how to fine-tune certain mind-receptors to the frequencies to these tiny transmissions can witness all events that have ever occurred; and this sacred recording can never be revised or edited. It was only a matter of time before someone would become strong enough to open our Father's Record Book. As God's Children, our souls grow stronger and wiser with each incarnation. Levi H. Dowling (1844–1911) attained enough strength and knowledge to open The Book of God's Remembrance. Levi became strong enough (and worthy enough) sometime after his fiftieth year on Earth. He gained the strength and know-how through many years of practicing all-night sessions of meditation, combined with fasting. After reaching his goal, he was able to focus his mind on particular persons, places and times, and clearly view ancient events – as if happening 'here and now'. Levi concentrated on just a small portion of

God's History Book; he focused on 'the little book' – that tiny part of world history that is the record of Jesus' life. Therefore, there is no longer any reason to wonder who Jesus was, or to speculate or debate what he said or did. His entire life-story is now available in the Aquarian Gospel, and anyone who wishes may read. During meditation, Levi was able to re-play events (as many times as necessary) in order to provide us with a perfect transcript. He spent many months transcribing the events he directly witnessed in 'The Book of God's Remembrance' (also called The Akashic Records). His original manuscript, entitled 'The Aquarian Age Gospel of Jesus, the Christ of the Piscean Age,' is widely published under the title, 'The Aquarian Gospel of Jesus the Christ,' and is commonly referred to as simply, 'The Aquarian Gospel.' Have other people verified the existence of the Akashic Records? Yes; people who are (authentic) psychics and remote viewers perform their remarkable feats because they are able to catch fleeting glimpses (or impressions) of our Father's sacred recording. Prophets and seers have been more successful – sometimes able to clearly view past events (and foresee future incidents); but Levi gained complete access to Nature's hidden portico. He is the first person in Earth's history to be granted full access to the Mystic Records of Time, with permission to write down what he witnessed. Anyone who reads the Aquarian Gospel carefully, sincerely and comprehensively will recognize its authenticity; and indeed, only those who read this book carefully, sincerely and comprehensively can recognize its authenticity, and know it is genuine. Levi's sacred transcription far outshines all previous books of divine origin. It is not filled with enigmas, secret codes and riddles; nor does it contain long, arduous passages that offer little insight. This sacred book is succinct. Levi did not mince words – each chapter gets right to the point. The parables are comprehensible, and the text is superbly plain and clear and easy to understand. Levi is the transcriber, but who is the author of the Aquarian Gospel? None other than Jesus, Christ Himself, wrote this book! How can this be? Jesus knew that every word he spoke and every act he performed was being recorded in The Book of God's Remembrance; and He knew that 1,800 years after his lifetime (in preparation for Christ's return), a man would be born into the world who would gain enough strength to open our Father's sacred Recording, and thereby become a direct eyewitness to all the events of Jesus' life; and he would transcribe a totally accurate and detailed account of his life and teachings. Therefore, except for the introductory chapters and some of the narrative, Jesus is the true author of the Aquarian Gospel. He wrote the book by living it. 'His-story' is inscribed on nature's tiny discs (smaller than atoms), which form 'the walls of time,' and Levi, through years of practicing meditation and fasting, discovered the 'password,' and he has viewed the mystic walls, and he has transcribed. Levi has given us the most precious book ever written. His publication paves the way for Christ again. Our Father knew Levi's soul was poised to develop enough strength to open His sacred Book of Records, and so He sent Levi to Earth at the proper time – as the Age of Pisces draws to a close (during these 'end times'), and as The Age of Aquarius (the 'new age') commences. Levi is a messenger sent from God. Furthermore, Jesus was well aware that, during his life on Earth, few people were prepared to comprehend and accept his precious message, and so he shared much of his profound wisdom and understanding with only a few; but now, vast multitudes of human souls on Earth are finally mature enough to comprehend and assimilate the deep truths He conveyed – concerning the nature of God, the nature of Man, and our relationship. Thus, by the hand of Levi, God has given us this new book of scripture, which contains the life and teachings of Jesus; and anyone who wishes, may now read and comprehend the deep, precious knowledge and wisdom (which our Lord shared with only a few 2,000 years ago). I suggest that anyone who doubts this is true is well advised to read this book (carefully and comprehensively) before he would suggest it is anything less than God's most recent Scriptural Gift to Mankind. It is a mistake to assume that God would never send us a new book of scripture.

So ends Michael O'Keefe's adulatory review.

It is not the purpose of this book to discuss the whole of the gospel's voluminous content, but to concentrate, single-mindedly, on our quest. For this reason I will render only sections V, VI and VII and Chapter 176 in Section XXI. In sections VI and VII, his adventures and teaching in India and Tibet are fully recounted. In section V, Dowling gives us his transcription from the Akashic records, or Book of God's Remembrance, of Jesus' childhood and early education. This section is important to us, not only as a precursor to his travels to India and Tibet, but also as the principle revelation Dowling received on the mysterious 'missing years' before Jesus left for India. He studied with the great Pharisaic Rabbi Hillel in the

Temple, and assisted his father as a carpenter. It is interesting to note that according to Levi's rendition, it was Mary who first introduced Jesus to the Hindu Vedas. Unfortunately for the contemporary reader, the language of the Aquarian Gospel is archaic and somewhat obscure, and broken up into biblical style verses without textual continuity. I have therefore decided, for ease of comprehension, to paraphrase the salient events central to our investigation from these three sections, including their different chapters, into a literary narrative in modern English. The later sections concern his adventures on his return journey through Persia, Assyria, Greece, and Egypt, then his ministry, trial, execution, resurrection, and eventual establishment of the Christine Church. While these may be of considerable interest to the general reader, and are portrayed in the film *The Aquarian Gospel* they are not germane to our central question. But chapter 176 of section XXI is apposite to our investigation. In this chapter, Dowling tells us that Jesus appears again, after the resurrection, to the Eastern sages in Prince Ravanna's palace in India, as a way of confirmation of his earlier visit. For those who wish to pursue these fascinating matters further, the Aquarian Gospel is still readily available in print. It is, however, impossible for us to form a considered judgement on the veracity of Dowling's revelation regarding his visit to India and Tibet without reading these actual sections, which are primarily concerned with this journey.

THE AQUARIAN GOSPEL SECTION V
Childhood and Early Education of Jesus

Joseph's house was on the Marmion Way in Nazareth. Here Mary taught her son the lessons to be learned from the Bible stories. The child Jesus also greatly loved the Vedic Hymns and the Avesta, but most of all he enjoyed King David's Psalms and the powerful words of King Solomon's wisdom. The prophetic books of Judaism were his delight, and when he was seven years old, he no longer needed the books to read, as he had remembered every word. Joachim and his wife, the grandparents of Jesus, provided a great feast in honour of the prodigious child, and their entire family were honoured guests. During the meal, Jesus stood up before the assembly and said, 'I had a dream, and in my dream I stood before the sea, on a sandy beach. The waves were high, and a great storm was raging. Someone from above handed me a wand. I held the wand and touched the sand, and every grain became a living thing. The whole beach was a wonderful mass of beauty and song. I touched the waters with my feet, and they changed to trees, flowers, singing birds, and everything was praising Almighty God. A voice spoke, whom I didn't see, and the voice said, "There is no death"!'

His grandmother Anna loved the child, she laid her hand on Jesus' head and said, 'I saw you stand beside the sea, I saw you touch the sand and waves, I saw them turn into living things and then I knew the dream's meaning. Your wand is the Truth. With this, you touch the multitudes, and every man becomes a messenger of holy light and life. You touch the waves upon the ocean of life, their turmoil ceases, the very winds become a song of praise. There is no death, because the wand of Truth can change the driest bones to living things, and bring forth beautiful flowers from stagnant ponds, and turn the most discordant musical notes to rapturous harmony and praise.'

Grandfather Joachim said, 'My son, today you pass the seventh milestone of your journey through life, and we shall give you, as a remembrance of your seventh birthday, whatever you desire. Choose that which will give you the most delight!'

Jesus replied, 'I do not want any gifts, for I am satisfied and content, but if I could make a multitude of children happy on this day, I would be greatly pleased. There are very many hungry boys and girls in Nazareth who would love to eat with us at this feast, and share all the pleasures of the day. The richest gift that you can give to me is your permission to go out and find these needy children, and bring them back here, so they may feast with us all.'

Joachim replied, 'It is well! Go out and find the poor boys and girls, and bring them here. We shall prepare enough food for them all.' Jesus did not wait one moment. He ran and entered every dingy hut and shack in the town. He did not waste words, but told them of this invitation everywhere. In a short time, 103 happy, ragged boys and girls followed him up the Marmion Way. The guests made room, the banqueting hall was filled with young Jesus' guests and both he and his mother helped to serve. There was sufficient food for everybody, and all were very glad. So this birthday gift of the young Jesus was a crown of righteousness.

Now Rabbi Barachia of the Nazareth Synagogue helped

Mary in her son's education. One Sabbath after the Synagogue service, the Rabbi said to Jesus, as he sat in silent meditation, 'Which is the greatest of the Ten Commandments?' Jesus replied, 'I don't see a greatest of the Ten Commandments. I see the golden chord that runs through all of the ten commands that binds them fast and makes them one. This cord is Love, and it belongs to every word of all the Ten Commandments. If one is full of love, he cannot kill, cannot testify falsely, cannot covet, can do nothing but to honour God and mankind. If one is full of love, he does not need commands of any kind.'

Rabbi Barachia replied, 'Your words are well seasoned with the salt of wisdom, from above. Who is the teacher who has opened up this truth to you?' Jesus replied, 'I do not know of any teacher who opened up this truth for me. It seems to me that truth was never closed, and that it was always open, for the truth is one, and available everywhere. If we open up the windows of our minds, the truth will enter, and make herself at home. The truth can find her way through any crevice, window or open door!' The Rabbi responded, 'Tell me what hand is strong enough to open up these windows and doors of the mind so truth can enter?' Jesus answered, 'It seems to me that Love, the golden cord that binds the Ten Commandments into one, is powerful enough to open any human door, so that truth can walk in and cause the heart to understand.'

Now that evening Jesus and his mother sat alone and Jesus said to her, 'The Rabbi seems to think that God is partial in his treatment of the sons of men, and that the Jews are favoured and we are blessed above all other men. I do not see how God can have His favourites and be just. Aren't the Samaritans, Greeks and Romans just as much the Holy One's children as are we Jews? I think we Jews have built a wall around ourselves, and we see nothing the other side of it. We do not know that flowers are blooming out there, that sowing and reaping times belong to everybody, not only to the Jews. It would surely be good if we could break these barriers down so that the Jews might see that God has other children that are just as greatly blest. I wish to go from Israel and meet my kin in the other countries of my Father's lands.'

The great Jewish Festival of Passover took place, so Joseph, Mary and their son, and many of their relations, went to Jerusalem. The boy was now ten years old. Jesus watched the butchers kill the lambs and birds and burn them on the sacrificial altar in the name of God. His tender heart was shocked at this display of cruelty. He asked the presiding priest, 'What is the purpose of this slaughter of the beasts and birds. Why do you burn their flesh before the Lord?' The priest answered, 'This is our sacrifice for sin. God has commanded us to do these things, and said that in these sacrifices, all our sins are blotted out.' Jesus replied, 'Will you be kind enough to tell us when God proclaimed that sins are blotted out by sacrifices of any kind? Didn't King David say that God requires a sacrifice for sin? That it is sin itself to bring before his face burnt offerings, as offerings for sin? Did not the prophet Isaiah say exactly the same?'

The priest answered, 'My child you are beside yourself. Do you know more about the laws of God than all the priests of Israel? This is no place for young boys to show off their cleverness.' Jesus ignored his taunts, but went to the famed Rabbi Hillel, head of the Sanhedrin and talked with him. He said, 'Rabbi, I wish to discuss with you. I am disturbed about this Passover festival. I thought the Temple was the house of God, where love and kindness dwell. Don't you hear the bleating of those lambs, the pleading of those doves, that the men are killing there? Don't you smell the awful stench that comes from burning flesh? Can a man be kind and just, and still be full of cruelty? A God that takes delight in sacrifice, in blood and burning flesh, is not my Father-God. I want to find a God of Love, and you my Master, you are wise, surely you can tell me where to find the God of Love?'

Hillel, however, could not find an answer for the boy. His heart was stirred with sympathy. He called the lad to him, he laid his hand upon his head and wept. He said, 'There is a God of love, you shall come with me, and hand in hand, we shall go forth and find the God of love.' Jesus then said, 'Why do we need to go anywhere? I thought that God is everywhere. Can't we purify our hearts and drive out cruelty, and every wicked thought, and create within a temple where the God of love can dwell?'

The Head of the great Sanhedrin felt as though he was himself the child, and that before him stood a rabbi, a master of the higher law. He said to himself, 'This child is surely a prophet sent from God.' He sought the boy's parents and asked that Jesus might live with them to learn the precepts of the law, and all the lessons of the Temple priests. Joseph and Mary gave their consent, and Jesus did live in the holy Temple in Jerusalem, and Rabbi Hillel taught him every day. So each day, Hillel also learned from Jesus many lessons of the higher life. The youth remained with Hillel for a whole year in the Temple, and then went back to his home in Nazareth, where he worked with Joseph as a carpenter.

Once more the great Passover Festival was on, so Joseph, Mary and Jesus went to the Temple in Jerusalem, once again. Jesus was now 12 years old, one year before his Bar Mitzvah confirmation. There were many Jews and converts from different countries present. Jesus sat among the priests and doctors of the law in the Temple hall.

The youth opened up a prophetic book and read, 'Woe, woe, to Ariel, the town where David dwelled! I will dismantle Ariel, and she shall groan and weep. I will camp against her round about with hostile posts; and I will bring her low and she shall speak out of the earth; with muffled voice like a familiar spirit shall she speak; yea, she shall only whisper forth her speech; and foes unnumbered like the grains of dust shall come upon her suddenly. The Lord of Hosts will visit her with thunder and with tempest, and with storm; with earthquake, and with devouring flames. Lo all these people have deserted me. They draw to me with speech, and with their lips they honour me; their hearts are far removed from me; their fear for me is that inspired by man. And I will breathe an adverse breath upon my people, Israel; the wisdom of their wise men shall be lost; the understanding of their prudent men shall not be found. My people seek to hide their counsel from the Lord, so that their works may not be seen. They fain would cover up their works with darkness of the night, and say, "Who sees us now? Who knows us now?" Poor foolish men! Shall that which has been made say of its maker, "He is naught, I made myself"? Or shall the pot say, "You have no skill; you do not know"? But this will not for ever be; the time will come when Lebanon will be a fruitful field, and fruitful fields will be transformed to groves. And on that day the deaf will hear the words of God; the blind will read the Book of God's Remembrance. And suffering ones will be relieved, and they will have abundant joy; and everyone that needs will be supplied; and it will come to pass that all the foolish will be wise. The people will return and sanctify the Holy One, and in their heart of hearts, lo, they will reverence him.'

When Jesus had finished reading, he set aside the book and said, 'You Masters of the Law, will you make plain for us the prophet's words?' Rabbi Hillel was there, and he rose and said, 'Perhaps our young Rabbi who has read the words will be the interpreter?' So Jesus replied, 'The Ariel of the prophet is our own Jerusalem. By selfishness and cruelty this people have become a stench unto Elohim. The prophet saw these days from afar, and it was of these times that he wrote these words. Our doctors, lawyers, priests and scribes oppress the poor, while they all live in luxury. The sacrifices and the offerings of Israel are but abominations unto God. The only sacrifice that God requires is one's self. Because of this injustice and this cruelty of man to man, the Holy One has spoken of this commonwealth, "Lo, I will overturn, yes, I will overturn, it shall be overturned, and it shall be no more until he comes whose right it is and I will give it unto him. In all the world there is one law of righteousness, and he who breaks that law will suffer grief; for God is just." For Israel has gone far astray; has not regarded justice, nor the rights of man, and God demands that Israel shall reform, and turn again to ways of holiness. If our people will not hear the voice of God, lo, nations from afar will come and sack Jerusalem, and tear our Temple down, and take our people captive into foreign lands. But this will not be forever; though they will be scattered far and wide, and wander here and there among the nations of the Earth, like sheep that have no shepherd. The time will come when God will restore the captives as hosts; for Israel shall return and dwell in peace. And after many years Solomon's Temple shall be built again, and the one in whom the pure in heart delights will come and glorify the house of God, and reign in righteousness.' When Jesus had finished speaking he stepped aside, and all the congregation were amazed and said, 'This surely is the Christ.'

The great Pesach Festival was over and the Nazarenes went journeying back to their homes. When they were in Samaria, Jesus suddenly disappeared, and Mary asked everybody where he was but nobody knew. Joseph asked all the family members, who were on their way to Galilee, but nobody knew. Then Joseph, Mary and a son of Zebedee searched the whole of Jerusalem, but he was nowhere to be found. They enquired at the Temple courts, and asked the guards if they had seen a fair-headed boy, with deep blue eyes, 12 years old, anywhere. 'Yes,' they replied, 'He is in the Temple now disputing with the Doctors of the Law.' So they entered and found him as the guards had said. Mary scolded Jesus, and said, 'Why do you treat your parents like this? We have searched for two whole days for you. We were very afraid you had come to some grievous harm.' Jesus answered and said, 'Don't you know that I must be about my Father's work?' He then went around the Temple hall and pressed every learned Doctor of the Law's hand, and said, 'I trust we shall meet again.'

Then he went back with his parents on their way to Nazareth, and when he reached home, he settled down again, assisting his father in his workshop. One day as he was fetching some tools, he said, 'These tools remind me of the ones we handle in the workshop of the mind, where things are made of thought, and whereby we build character. We use the square to measure all our lines, to straighten out the crooked places on the way, and make the corners of our conduct perfect. We use the compass to draw a circle around our passions and desires to keep them within the boundaries of righteousness. We use an axe to cut away the knotty, useless and ungainly parts, and make our characters symmetrical. We use the hammer to drive home the truth, and pound it in, until it is a part of every part. We use the plane to smooth the rough, uneven surfaces of joint, block and board that go to build our inner temple of truth. The chisel, line, plummet and saw all have their uses in the workshop of the mind. And then this ladder with its threefold steps, faith, hope and love, we use to climb up to the dome of purity in life. And there on a 12-step ladder we ascend until we reach the pinnacle of that which life should be spent to build – the Temple of Perfected Man.'

SECTION VI
The Life and Works of Jesus in India

The Royal Prince, Ravanna of Orissa, southern India, was a man of considerable wealth, with a notable reputation for administering impartial and fair justice. With a party of learned Brahmin priests, he once decided to visit Jerusalem, in order to study the wisdom of the West. He chanced, one day, to be in the main Temple, when the young Jesus was there to discuss points of the Torah with the most senior rabbis of the day. As Jesus discoursed among them, Ravanna was stunned with amazement by the lad's erudition and wisdom. He enquired of the famed Rabbi Hillel who this prodigious lad was, where he came from, and what he represented in his eyes.

Hillel informed Ravanna that the rabbis call this child 'The Day Star From on High', because he has been sent to bring a light, the light of life, to enlighten mankind's way and redeem his people, Israel. Hillel told Prince Ravanna as much as he knew about the boy, about the biblical prophecies concerning him, about the miracles of the night when he was born in a stable, and the visitation by Magi priestly kings. He also told him of his divine protection from King Herod's wrath, his escape into Egypt, and how he served his father the carpenter Joseph in Nazareth.

Ravanna was enchanted and asked about the most direct route to Nazareth that he might go and honour such a one, whom he saw as a son of God. So with the full panoply of his sumptuous train he travelled to Nazareth near Galilee. There he found the young Jesus working, engaged in building dwellings for the needy. He was climbing a 12-step ladder carrying a compass, a carpenter's square and an axe.

Ravanna could not resist shouting loudly, 'All hail, most favoured son of heaven!' There and then, Ravanna decided to arrange a feast for all the townsfolk at the inn where he was to stay. He held a feast at which Jesus and his parents Joseph and Mary were the honoured guests. To reciprocate Joseph invited the Prince to spend some days with his family, in their house in Marmion Way. Ravanna was determined to learn the secret of his son's wisdom, but it was beyond Joseph's comprehension to explain it too him.

Ravanna asked that he might become the child's patron and take him on a journey to the East where he might learn the knowledge and teachings of the Brahmins. Jesus was enthusiastic to accept the invitation, and after some time Joseph and Mary gave their consent.

So Ravanna with his companions began their journey to India, along the fabled Silk Route, and after several days arrived at the River Sind, which they crossed, and on to Orissa where they went to the Prince's palace. The Brahmins were pleased to see the return of their beloved Ravanna, and with delight received the Jewish lad who was to be their pupil. He was accepted to study in the famed Jagannath Temple and be taught the Sacred Vedas and the Laws of Manu. His Brahmin teachers were astounded at his clear conception of the ancient texts, and were even more amazed when he was able to comment on the subtle meanings of these scriptures.

Among the Jagannath priests was a Brahmin named Lamaas who greatly admired the boy, and one day while walking, encountered the lad and said, 'My young Jewish master – what is Truth?'

Jesus answered, 'The Truth is changeless. In the whole world there are two principles, one is Truth and the other is Falsehood. Truth is "what is" and Falsehood is that which only "appears to be". Truth is the All, which has no cause, yet is the cause of everything. Falsehood is nothing. Whatever has been created will be dissolved. All beginnings have an end. All that is seen is only a reflection of the All and therefore nothing, and must eventually pass away. The objects we see are mere reflections, just appearances, while the ether vibrates, in such and such a way, and when conditions alter they disappear. The Holy Spirit is Truth, and is that which was, is, and evermore shall be; it cannot change or pass away.'

Lamaas said, 'You have answered well, now what is man?'

Jesus replied, 'Man is a strange admixture of Truth and Falsehood. He is the spirit made flesh, so Truth and Falsehood are conjoined. When they strive one against the other, Falsehood is defeated and man as Truth abides.'

Lamaas then asked, 'What do you say about Power?'

Jesus replied, 'Power is God's will and is all powerful. It is that which will manifest, directed by the Holy Spirit. There is power in the winds, the seas, lightning, human strength and sight. Thought of God directs these forces until they have completed their work.'

Then Lamaas asked what he would say about Understanding. Jesus said, 'It is the rock on which man builds himself, it is the gnosis of the All and of the Naught. It is knowledge of the lower self, the sensual realization of man's own powers.'

Then Lamaas asked about Wisdom. Jesus replied, 'It is the Pure Consciousness that knows Man is the All, and that God and Man are One; that falsehood is falsehood; power is an illusion; heaven, hell and earth are not above, around, or below, but inside man himself; which in the light of the All becomes the naught, and God is the All.'

Lamaas then asked about Faith. Jesus said, 'Faith is the certainty of God's omnipotence and Man's, the surety that he can reach the divine life. Salvation is the ladder reaching from the heart of man to the heart of God. The three steps are belief; that is what man thinks is truth. Then faith, this is what he knows to be truth. Then fruition is last, when man himself becomes the truth. Belief is lost in faith, man is saved when he reaches the divine, when he and God become One.'

Then Jesus with his new friend Lamaas travelled through Orissa, and the Ganges Valley, seeking wisdom from the common folk, the untouchables, the merchants and the masters. They stayed in Benares where Jesus sought to learn the Hindu arts of medicine, and became a pupil of Udraka, the foremost of the Hindu healers. Udraka taught him the uses of herbs, heat and cold, sunlight and darkness. He said that the laws of nature were the laws of health, and transgressions of these laws led to illness. Obedience to the laws of nature resulted in bodily equilibrium. Harmony was health, disease was discord. The body was like a harp, and when the strings were too tight or too loose, the body was out of tune. Man may exercise his will to relax or tighten the strings as needed. When man has faith in God, in Nature and himself, he knows the Word of Power, which is balm for every wound, and a cure for all ills. The healer is the man who inspires faith. Souls are reached by souls that speak to souls. What suits one may many not suit another. There are evil spirits which cause illness and discord. The true healer, by force of will, can vanquish these demonic spirits. He also has helpers in the higher realms that will aid in exorcism.

Jesus bowed his head in recognition of this Master Soul, and went on his way. He stayed in the Jagannath Temple for four whole years. One day sitting among the priests he enquired about the system of castes and asked, 'Why do you not say that all men are equal in the sight of God?'

An elder Brahmin replied, 'The Holy One, whom we call Brahman, created men according to his will, and men should not complain about their destiny.

'Four men stood before Brahman at the time of world creation. Four men stood before him. One came from Brahman himself, and was white, he was like Brahman and was called a Brahmin. He was raised high, and stood above all needs, he had no need to labour. He was named the priest of Brahman, the holy one to act for Him in all earthly affairs. The second man was red. He was called the Warrior. He was destined to be the king, the ruler and the soldier whose highest duty was protection of the priests.

'The third man came and he was yellow in colour. He was named the Merchant, and it was his duty to farm, and to be responsible for commerce. The fourth man was black. He was called the Untouchable, whose duty it was to be the servant of mankind, without the rights of the others, or access to the holy scriptures, and be in a state of servitude to the other castes.'

Then Jesus spoke and said, 'This Brahman is not a god of justice and of righteousness, for he has exalted one and brought another low.' He said no more but lifted up his eyes to heaven and prayed, 'My Father, God, who was, is and evermore shall be, within Thy hands are the scales of justice and righteousness. Who in Thy boundlessness of love has created all men to be equal in Thy sight, so all can look up equally to Thy Name and say our Father. I praise Thee.'

The Brahmins, hearing his prayer, were angry and seized him in such a way that could have done him bodily harm. But Lamaas intervened and said, 'You Brahmins, beware, you know not what you do! Wait until you know the God this youth adores! I have seen this youth at prayer, when a halo of golden light surrounded him. Beware! His God may be more powerful than Brahman. If Jesus speaks the truth, you cannot force him to desist, if he is wrong and you are right, his words will come to naught. For right is might, and in the end shall prevail!' Then the Brahmins refrained from harming Jesus, but one spoke out saying, 'Within this holy place has not this reckless youth done violence to Brahman? The law is plain: it says, "He who reviles the name of Brahman shall die"!'

Then Lamaas pleaded for Jesus' life; and the Brahmins merely took a scourge of cords and drove him out of the temple. So Jesus went his way and took refuge with the merchants and untouchables. To them he declared the doctrine of equality. He told them of the Brotherhood of Man and the Fatherhood of God. These common folk listened with delight, and learned to pray 'Our Father who art in heaven'.

When Jesus saw the untouchables, the farmers and merchants in such vast numbers, drawing near to hear his words, he told them a new parable. He said, 'Once there was a great nobleman who owned a large estate. He had four sons, and he wished that all would grow up to be strong by standing tall, and using all the talents that God had given them.

'So he gave each one a share of his wealth and told them to go, each on his own way. The eldest was very self-centred, ambitious, cunning, and could think very quickly. He said to himself, "I am the eldest son, and therefore my brothers should become servants at my feet." So he summoned them, and one he made the puppet ruler, gave him arms, and told him he must defend the whole estate. To the next he gave the use of all the land, the wells, the flocks of sheep and herds of cattle. He instructed him to bring him the best of all his gains. To the youngest he said, "You are the youngest son, the rest of the estate has now been assigned, you have no part or place in anything here." Then he took a chain and cruelly bound his brother to a bare rock in the desert and said to him, "You have been born a slave without any rights, you must rest here contented with your lot, as there is no release for you until you die and leave the body."

'After a certain time, the day of reckoning came. The nobleman called up his sons to render their accounts. When he found out that his eldest son had seized the whole estate and made his brothers slaves, he seized him, stripped him of his Brahmin robes and threw him into a dungeon, where he was forced to stay until he atoned for all the wrongs he had done to the others. Then, as though they were children's toys he tossed in the air the throne and armour of the puppet ruler, and locked him up in a prison cell. Then he called his farmer son and asked him why he hadn't rescued his younger brother, chained up in the desert? When the son didn't answer he took away all his flocks, herds, fields and wells. He sent him out to the desert, until he too had atoned for all he had done. Then he went to where the youngest son was chained and freed him, telling his son to go in peace. Now when the sons had all paid their debts of contrition, they were summoned before him to stand before the bar of justice. They had all learned their lessons well, so the father again divided his estate. He gave each an equal share, and told them to respect the laws of equity and righteousness, and dwell in peace.'

Then an untouchable spoke up and said, 'May we who are but slaves, cut down like beasts to satisfy the whims of the priests – may we have hope that someone will come to break our chains and set us free?'

Jesus said, 'The untouchables shall be as free as the priests. The farmers and merchants shall walk hand in hand with the King, for all the world will possess the brotherhood of man. So men, arise! Be fully conscious of your powers, for he who wills it, need not remain a slave. Just live as you would your brother live; unfold each day like the lily of the field, for the Earth is yours, and God will bring you all to your own.'

Then all the people cried, 'Show us the way so that like the lily of the field we may unfold and come unto our own!'

In every city in Orissa, Jesus taught the people. At Katak, by the riverside, thousands came to follow him. One day a juggernaut of Jagannath was hauled along by scores of frenzied men. Jesus said, 'Behold a form without a spirit passes by, a body without a soul, a temple without altar fires. This juggernaut of Lord Krishna is an empty vehicle, for Lord Krishna isn't there! This carriage is an idol of a people drunk on the wine of carnal lust! God doesn't live in the babble of tongues, there is no way to reach Him from an idol shrine. God's meeting place with man is in the heart, and He speaks with a still small voice, and he who hears is silent.'

Then the people said, 'Teach us to know the Holy One who speaks within the heart, the God of the still, small voice.'

Jesus said, 'The Holy Spirit cannot be seen by mortal eyes, nor can man ever see the Spirit of the Holy One. Yet in their image, man is created, and he who looks into the face of a man or woman, looks at the image of their God who speaks within.

'When man honours man, he honours God, and what man does for man, he does for God. You must bear in mind that when man harms in thought, or word or deed another man, he wrongs God.

'If you would serve the God who speaks within the heart, just serve your next of kin, and those that are not kin, the stranger at your gates, the foe who seeks to do you harm. Help the poor and the weak. Harm no one, and don't envy that which isn't yours. Then with your own tongue the Holy One shall speak, and he will smile behind your tears, will light your countenance with joy, and fill your hearts with peace.'

Then the people asked, 'To whom shall we bring gifts? Where shall we offer sacrifices?' Jesus replied, 'Our Father doesn't ask for needless waste of plants, doves, or lambs. That which you burn on any altar, you throw away. No blessing can be bestowed on anyone who takes food from hungry mouths to be destroyed by fire. When you would offer sacrifices to God, just take your gift of grain or meat and lay it on a poor man's table. From that, an incense will arise to heaven, which shall return to you with blessedness. Tear down your idols, they can't hear you! Turn all your sacrificial altars into fuel for the flames. Instead, make human hearts your altars, and burn your sacrifices with the fire of love.' And all the people were overawed, and would have worshipped Jesus as a god; but Jesus said, 'I am your brother, a man who has just come to show the way to God; you shall not worship man; praise God, the Holy One!'

The fame of Jesus as a teacher spread through all the land, and people flocked from near and far to hear his words of truth. He taught at Behar, by the sacred river of the Brahmins, for many days. There, Ach, a wealthy citizen of Behar, honoured him with a feast, and invited everyone to come. Many did come, including thieves, extortionists and prostitutes. Jesus sat down with them and taught, but some who followed him were aggrieved because of the company he kept. They upbraided him and said, 'Rabbi, master of the wise, this day shall be an evil one for you. The news will spread that you consort with prostitutes and thieves, and men will shun you like they shun an asp!'

Jesus answered them saying, 'A Master never hides himself for the sake of reputation or fame. These are worthless baubles of the day. They rise and sink, like empty bottles on a stream. They are illusions and will pass away.

They are emblems of what the thoughtless think, the noise that the noisy make, for shallow men judge by their own shallowness!

'God and all Masters judge men and women by what they truly are, and not what by what they seem to be; neither by their reputation nor their fame!

'These thieves and prostitutes are all children of my Father. Their souls are just as precious in His sight as yours, or those of the Brahmin priests. They are working out the same destinies that you, who pride yourselves on your so-called respectability and moral worth, are also working out. Some of them have solved much harder problems than you have solved, you men who regard them with scorn! Yes, they are sinners, but confess their guilt, while you are guilty, but are hypocritical enough to wear a polished appearance to mask your guilt.

'Suppose you men and women who scorn these prostitutes, drunkards and thieves, who know that you are pure at heart and in life, that you are morally superior to them, stand up that we may know just who you are!

Sin lies in the wish, the desire, not in the deed. You covet other people's wealth, you look at beautiful bodies, and deep within your hearts you lust after them! You practise deceit every day, and crave gold, honour and fame for your own selfish selves! The man or woman who covets is a thief, and she or he who lusts is a prostitute. You whom are none of these, speak out!'

Nobody spoke out, the accusers held their peace.

Then Jesus said, 'The pure in heart never accuse. The vile in heart who desire to cover up their guilt with the holy smoke of piety are ever loathing the drunkards, thieves and prostitutes! This loathing and scorn is a mockery, for if the tinselled coat of reputation could be torn away, the loud protestor would be found to be revelling in his lust, deceit and many forms of secret sin. The man who spends his time in pulling out other people's weeds can have no time to pull out his own, and all the choicest blooms of life will soon be choked and die, and nothing will remain but darnel, thistles, and burs.'

Now Jesus told them another beautiful parable. He said, 'A farmer owned fine fields of fully ripened grain, but when he looked at the crop, he saw that the blades of many of the stalks of wheat were bent and broken. So when he sent his reapers into the field he said, "We will not save the stalks of wheat that have the broken blades. Go, cut and burn the stalks with broken blades!" After some days he went to inspect his grain, but he couldn't find even a single kernel. So he summoned the harvesters and asked them where was his grain? They replied, "We followed your orders, we gathered up and then burned the stalks with broken blades, and not a stalk was left to take into the barn." So I am telling you all, if God saves only those who have no broken blades, who have been perfect in his sight, who will be saved?'

After hearing this parable, his accusers hung their heads in shame, and Jesus proceeded on his way.

Benares is the sacred city of the Brahmins, and he taught there. He was hosted by Udraka who arranged a feast in his honour, and many high-born Brahmin priests and scribes were invited. Jesus addressed them saying, 'It is with great delight that I speak to you all concerning life and the brotherhood of life. Our universal God is One, yet He is more than One. Everything is God; all things are One. Through the sweet spirit of God, all life is bound in Oneness; so if you touch a fibre of any living thing, you send a vibration from the centre to the outer limits of life. And when you crush beneath your foot the meanest worm, you shake God's throne, and cause His sword of righteousness to tremble in its sheath. The bird sings its song for mankind, and men vibrate in unison to help it sing. The ant builds his home, the bee its sheltering hive, the spider weaves her web, and the flowers breathe to them a spirit in their fragrance that gives them the strength to work. Men, worms, birds, beasts and creeping things are deities made flesh, so how dare men kill any creature? It is cruelty that makes the world crookedly askew. When men have learned that whenever they harm a living creature they harm themselves, they surely won't kill, nor cause a creature that God has made, to suffer pain.'

A lawyer then asked, 'I pray you, Jesus, tell us who is this God you speak about? Where are His priests, His temples and His shrines?'

Jesus answered, 'The God I speak about is everywhere; He cannot be enclosed by walls, nor hedged with boundaries of any kind. All people worship God the One, but they don't all see Him alike. This universal God is wisdom, will and love. All men don't see this Triune God. One sees Him as the God of might, another as the God of reason, another as the God of love. A man's ideal is his God, and so, as man unfolds, his God unfolds. Man's God today or tomorrow is not God. The nations of the Earth see God from different standpoints, so He doesn't seem the same to all. Man names the attribute of God he sees, and this to him is all of God; and every nation sees a part of God, and every nation has a different name for God. You Brahmins call Him Parabrahman, in Egypt He is Thoth, in Greece He is Zeus, Jehovah is His Hebrew name; but everywhere He is the causeless Cause, the rootless Root from which all things have grown.

'When men become afraid of God and take Him for a foe, they dress each other in fancy garbs and call them priests. They charge them to restrain the wrath of God by prayers, and when they fail to win His favour by their petitions, they try to buy Him off with the sacrifice of an animal or a bird. When man sees God as One with him, as their Father-God, he needs no intermediary, no priest to intercede. He goes straight to Him and says, my Father-God! And then he lays his hand in God's own hand and all is well. And that is God. Each one of you is a priest, just for yourself, God does not want the sacrifice of blood. Just dedicate your life in sacrificial service to the All of life, and God is well pleased.'

When Jesus had said all this, he stood aside. The guests were amazed, but argued amongst themselves. Some claimed he was inspired by Holy Brahman, while others said he was insane, and others said he was obsessed and that he spoke as the devils speak.

But Jesus did not wait. Among the guests was a tiller of the soil, a generous soul, a seeker after truth, who loved the words that Jesus spoke, so Jesus left with him, and stayed in his home.

Among Benares' temple priests was one, a guest named Ajainin, from Lahore. Through merchants, he heard about the Jewish youth, and about his words of wisdom; so he travelled to see the lad, and hear him speak. The Brahmin priests did not accept the truths that Jesus brought, and were angered by much of what he had said at Udraka's feast. Nevertheless they wished to know more about the boy, and hear him speak, so they invited him to temple. Jesus told them, 'The Light is most abundant, and it shines for all; if you would know the Light, come to the Light. If you would hear the message that the Holy One has given to me to give to mankind, come to me.'

Now when the priests heard what Jesus had to say, they became enraged. Ajainin didn't share their wrath, and he sent a messenger with costly gifts to Jesus at the farmer's house with this message. 'I pray to you, Master, listen to my words. The Brahmin's law forbids that any priest should enter the home of one of low estate, but you can come to us, and I am sure these priests will hear you speak. I hope you will come and dine with us today.' Jesus replied saying, 'The Holy One regards all men alike. The dwelling of my host is good enough for any council of the sons of men. If pride of caste keeps you away, you are unworthy of the Light. My Father-God does not regard man-made laws. Your gifts I return, you cannot buy the knowledge of the Lord with gold, or precious presents.' These words angered the priests more and more, so they began to plot and plan how they may drive him out of the country. Ajainin did not join them in their plotting, he left the temple that night, and came to the house where Jesus stayed. Then Jesus said, 'There is not any night when the sun shines. I have no secret messages to give. In the Light all secrets are revealed.'

Ajainin said, 'I came all the way from Lahore that I might learn about your ancient wisdom and this kingdom of the Holy One of which you speak. Where is the kingdom? Where is the King? Who are subjects and what are its laws?'

Jesus replied, 'This kingdom is not far away, but man with his mortal eyes cannot see it for it lies within his heart. You need not seek the King in earth, sea or sky, he is not there, yet he is everywhere. He is the Christ of God, universal love. The gate of this dominion is not high, and he who enters it must fall down on his knees. It is not wide, but none can carry sensual, fleshy, carnal bundles through that gate. The lower self must be transmuted into the Spirit Self. The body must be cleansed in living streams of purity.'

Ajainin asked, 'Can I become a subject of that King?' Jesus replied, 'You are yourself a king, and you may enter through the gate and be a subject of the King of kings. But you must set aside your priestly robes, must cease to serve the Holy One for payment in gold. You must give your life, and all you have, in willing service to the sons of men.'

Jesus said no more, and Ajainin left. Although he could not comprehend the truth that Jesus said, he saw what he had never seen before. The realm of faith had never been explored by him, but in his heart, the seeds of faith and universal brotherhood had found good soil. As he travelled home, he seemed to sleep, to pass through the darkest night, and when he awoke the Sun of Righteousness had arisen. He had found the King. So, in Benares, Jesus stayed for many days and taught the people.

One day as Jesus stood beside the Ganges, busy with his work, a caravan returning from the west drew near. Approaching him, a member said, 'We have just come to you from your native land and bring unwelcome news. Your father is no longer on Earth and your mother grieves. None are able to comfort her. She wonders whether you are still alive or not as she longs to see you again.' Jesus bowed his head in silent thought. Then he wrote a letter and this is what he said. 'My mother, noblest of woman-kind. A man from my native land has brought me word that father is no longer in the body, and that you grieve, and are disconsolate. My mother, all is very well, is well for father, and is well for you! His work in this "earth round" is over, and it was nobly done. In all walks of life, no man can charge him with deceit, dishonesty, or wrong intent. Here in this life, he completed many laborious tasks, and he has left us, prepared to solve the problems of this "round of soul". Our Father-God is with him there, as he was with him here, and his angel guards his footsteps in case he goes astray. Why should you weep? Tears cannot conquer grief. There is no power in grief to mend a broken heart. The plane of grief is idleness; the busy soul can never grieve; it has no time for grief. When grief comes trooping through the heart, just lose yourself by plunging deeply into the ministry of love, and grief vanishes. Yours is a ministry of love, and the whole world is calling out for love. Let the past go with the past. Rise from the cares of mundane concerns, and give your life for those who live. Furthermore, if you should lose your life in serving life, you will be sure to find in it the morning sun, the evening dews, the song of birds, the beauty of flowers by day, and the stars by night. In a short while your cares of this "earth round" will all be solved, and when your sums are all worked out it will be unalloyed joy for you to enter wider fields of usefulness, and solve the greater problems of the soul. Strive then to be contented, and I shall come to you some day and bring you richer gifts than gold or precious stones. I am sure that John will care for you, supplying all your needs; and I am always with you. Jehoshua.' So by the hand of a merchant, travelling to Jerusalem, he sent this letter on its way.

The words and works of Jesus caused considerable unrest throughout the country. The common folk were his friends, believed in him, and followed him in throngs. The priests and rulers were afraid of him, his very name sent terror to their hearts. He preached the brotherhood of life, the righteousness of equal right for all, and taught the uselessness of priests and sacrificial rites. He shook the very foundations on which the Brahmin's system stood. He made the Brahmin idols seem so petty, sacrifice fraught with sin, so that shrines and prayer wheels were all forgotten. The priests declared that if this Hebrew youth should stay any longer in the land, there would be a revolution. The common people would rise up, kill the priests and destroy the temples. So they sent a summons around and about, and the priests from every province assembled. Benares became on fire with Brahmin zeal.

Lamaas from the temple Jagannath, who knew the inner life of Jesus well, was in their midst, and heard the rantings of the priests. He stood up and said, 'My brother priests, take care, this is an important day. The world is watching, the very life of Brahmin thought is now on trial. If we are blind to reason and prejudice rules so that we resort to brutish force, and dye our hands in the blood of one that may, in the sight of Brahman, be innocent and pure, his vengeance may fall down on us! The very rock on which we stand may shatter beneath our feet, and our beloved priesthood, our laws and shrines will fall into decay!'

His fellow priests refused to allow him to continue. They rushed up and beat him, spat on him, and called him a traitor. They threw him out of the temple and he lay bleeding in the street. Then confusion reigned; the priests became an unruly mob. The sight of human blood led to fiendish acts and called for more. The rulers, fearing war, looked for Jesus, and found him calmly preaching in the market place. They urged him to leave, so he might save his life, but he refused to go. Then the priest tried to find a cause to arrest him, but he had not committed any crime. So false charges were preferred. But when the soldiers went to arrest him and take him to the Judgement Hall, they were afraid, because the people stood in his defence. The priests were perplexed, and decided to take his life by stealth. They found a man who was a murderer by trade, and sent him out by night to slay him. But Lamaas heard about this plot and sent a messenger to warn Jesus, who decided it was best to leave. That night he left Benares and hastily journeyed north. Everywhere he went, the farmers, merchants and untouchables helped him on his way. After many days he reached the foothills of the mighty Himalayas and rested in the city of Kapivastu. There the Buddhist priests opened wide their temple doors to receive him.

Among the Buddhist priests, there was one who perceived the truth in the words of wisdom that Jesus uttered. His name was Barata Arabo. Together they studied the Psalms of David and the Prophetical Books. They also read the Vedas, the Zoroastrian Avesta and the wisdom of Gautama Buddha. So they read about and discussed the possibilities of mankind.

Barata said, 'Man is the marvel of the universe. He is a part of the whole, for he has been a living being, on every plane of life. Time was, when man did not exist, he was merely formless substance in the moulds of time, then a protoplast. By universal law, all things evolve towards a state of perfection. That protoplast evolved, becoming worm, then reptile, bird and animal. Then finally it reached the form of man. Now man himself is "mind", and "mind" is here to attain perfection through experience. "Mind" is often manifest in fleshly form, best suited to its development. So "mind" may manifest as worm, bird, animal or man. The time shall come when the whole of life will be evolved up to the state of perfect man. Then after man, is man in perfection, he will evolve to even higher forms of life.'

Then Jesus questioned him and asked, 'Barata Arabo, who taught you this, that "mind" which is the man, may manifest in animal flesh, bird or creeping thing?'

Barat replied, 'From time immemorial our priests have told us so, and so we know.'

Jesus said, 'Enlightened Arabo, are you a mastermind, and do not know that man knows nothing by being told? Man may believe what others say, but this way he never knows. If man would know, he must himself become what he knows!

'Do you remember, Arabo, when you were an ape, a bird
or a worm? Now if you have no better proof of your supposition, than what the priests have told you, you do not really
know! You only guess. Take no notice then of what any man
has said. Let us forget the flesh and go with the mind into
the land of fleshless things; mind never forgets. Backward
through the ages masterminds can trace their origins, and
so they know. Time never was when man was not. That
which begins will have an end. If man was not, the time will
come when he will not exist. From God's own Record Book
we read, "The Triune God breathed forth, and seven spirits
stood before his face. The Hebrews call these spirits Elohim
and these are they who, in their boundless power created
everything that is or was. These spirits of the Triune God
moved on the face of boundless space and seven ethers there
were, and every ether had its form of life. These forms of life
were the thoughts of God, clothed in the substance of their
ethereal plane, and all the forms of life. Because all forms of
life on every plane are thoughts of God, all creatures think,
and every creature is possessed of will, and in its measure,
has the power to choose. And in their native planes all
creatures are supplied with nourishment from the ethers of
their planes. Men call these ether planes the planes of
protoplast, of earth, of plant, of animal, of man, of angel
and of cherubim. These planes, with all their teeming
thoughts of God, are never seen by the eyes of man in the
flesh. They are composed of substance far too fine for fleshly
eyes to see, and still they constitute the soul of things. And
with the eyes of soul all creatures see these ether planes, and
all the forms of life. And so it was with every living thing

until the will became a sluggish will, and then the ethers of the protoplast, the earth, the plant, the beast, the man, began to vibrate very slowly. The ethers all became denser, and all the creatures of these planes were clothed with coarser garbs, the garbs of flesh, which men can see; and so this coarser manifestation which men call 'physical', appeared. And this is what is called 'the Fall of Man', but man fell not alone, for protoplast, and earth, and plant and beast were all included in the fall. The angels and the cherubim did not fall, their wills were always strong, so they held the ethers of their planes in harmony with God. Now when the ethers reached the rate or numerical proportion of the atmosphere, as all the creatures of these planes must obtain their food from the atmosphere, the conflict came. Then that which the finite man has called 'survival of the fittest' became a law.

"'The stronger ate the bodies of the weaker manifestations, and here is where the carnal law of evolution had its rise. Now man in his utter shamelessness, strikes down and eats animal flesh, the animal eats the plant, the plant thrives on the soil, the earth absorbs the protoplast. The Kingdom of the Soul beyond this carnal evolution is unknown, and the great work of masterminds is to restore the birthright or heritage of man, to return him back to the estate which he has lost, when he will live again upon the ethers of his native plane. The thoughts of God do not change. The manifestations of life on every plane unfold into the perfection of their kind. So as the thoughts of God can never die, there is no death for any being of the seven ethers of the seven spirits of the Triune God. Thus soil can never be a plant, nor an animal, bird, nor reptile ever be man. The time will come when all these seven manifestations will be absorbed, and man and animal, plant, earth and protoplast will be redeemed."'

Barata was amazed; the Gnostic wisdom of this Jewish sage was a revelation! While Jesus was speaking, Vidyapati, wisest of the Indian sages, head of Kapavistu Temple, heard Barata speak to Jesus about man's origin, and heard the response of the Hebrew prophet. He spoke to all the priests of Kapavistu. 'Listen! We stand today upon a crest of time. Six times in the past a master soul was born, who gave glorious light to mankind. Now such a master sage stands here in Temple Kapavistu! This Hebrew prophet is the rising star of wisdom deified. He brings to us a knowledge of God's secrets. All the world shall hear his words and will pay attention to him, and glorify his name. You priests of Temple Kapavistu, stay! Be still and listen when he speaks. He is the Living Oracle of God.' Then all the priests gave thanks and praised the Buddha of Enlightenment.

Jesus sat beside a flowing spring, in silent meditation. It was a festival, and many untouchables were nearby. Jesus saw the hard-drawn lines of toil on every brow, and in every hand. There was no look of joy in any face. Not one of all the group could think of anything but their hard labour. Jesus spoke to one man and asked, 'Why you are all so sad? Have you no happiness in life?'

The man replied, 'We scarcely know the meaning of that word. We toil to live, and can hope for nothing else but toil, and bless the day when we can cease, and lay ourselves down to rest in Buddha's city of the dead.' Jesus' heart was moved to compassion and with love for these poor labourers said, 'Toil should not make a person feel sad. Men should be happiest when they work. When hope and love are behind the work, then all life is full of joy and peace, and that is heaven. Do you not know that such a heaven is for you?'

The man answered, 'We have heard of heaven, but then it is so far away, and we must live so many lives before we reach that place!'

Jesus said, 'My brother, your thoughts are wrong, your heaven is not far away, and it is not a place of measurement and boundaries, nor is it a country to be reached, it is a state of mind. God never made a heaven for man nor a hell. We are creators, and we make our own. Now cease to seek for heaven in the sky; just open wide the windows of your hearts, and like a flood of light, a heaven will come and bring a boundless joy; then work will not be a cruel task.' The people were astonished and came closer to hear this strange young master speak, imploring him to tell them more about his Father-God, and about the heaven that men can make on Earth, and about the boundless joy.

Then Jesus told them a parable. 'A certain man owned a field with poor, hard soil. In spite of constant toil, he could barely provide enough food to keep his family alive. One day a gifted miner, who could detect metals beneath the soil, passed by and saw the poor farmer and his infertile land. He called the weary peasant over and said, "My brother, do you know that I am certain that just below the surface of your barren field, rich treasures are concealed? You plough, sow, and reap in a scanty way, but day by day you are treading upon a mine of gold and precious stones.

This wealth does not lie upon the surface of the ground, but if you will dig away the rocky soil, and delve down deeply into the earth, you will no longer need to till the soil for such little reward." The man trusted his judgement and believed him. He thought, "This man surely knows, I will do what he says, and find these treasures." So he dug and dug away into the rocky soil, and deep down he found a mine of gold.' Then Jesus said, 'The poor sons of men are toiling hard on desert plains, burning sands and rocky soils. Are they doing what their fathers did, not dreaming they could do something better with the land? Behold, a master comes, and tells them of hidden wealth, that lies beneath the carnal flesh, treasures that no man can count. That deep in the heart, the richest gems abound, and that he who wills may open up the door and find them all.'

When the people heard this parable they said, 'Make known to us the way that we may find the wealth that lies deep in the heart.' Jesus opened up the way for them, and the labourers saw another side of life, and toil became a joy.

Next day there was a gala in sacred Kapavistu. A crowd of Buddhist worshippers met to celebrate a jubilee. Priests and masters from all parts of India were there. They taught, but embellished little truth with very many words. When Jesus went into the public square, he also taught, and spoke about his Father-Mother-God and the brotherhood of life. The priests and all the people were astounded at his words and said, 'Has the Buddha come again in the flesh? No one else could speak with such simplicity and power!'

Then Jesus gave another parable. He said, 'There was a neg-lected vineyard, all badly maintained. The vines were high and not pruned, the growth of leaves and branches was out of control. The broad leaves shut out the sunlight from the vines. The very few, small grapes were sour. One day a pruner came and, with his sharp knife, cut off every branch, and not a leaf remained, leaving just the root and stalk and nothing more. The busy neighbours came round and were amazed, and said to the pruner, "You foolish man, you have over-pruned, and the vineyard is spoiled. What desolation! There's no beauty left, and when harvest time comes, the gatherers will find no fruit." The pruner replied, "Content yourselves with whatever you may think, but come again at harvest time and watch!" So when harvest time came round, the busy neighbours came again and were amazed. The naked stalks had sprouted leaves and branches, and heavy clusters of delicious grapes weighed down every vine. The gatherers rejoiced, as every day they carried the rich fruitage to be pressed.' Then Jesus paused, before he spoke again to his rapt audience, 'Behold the vineyard of the Lord! His earth is spread with human vines. The exotic forms and rites of men are the branches, and their many leaves are merely words. They have grown so great that light no longer reaches the heart, and there is no fruit. Then a pruner comes, and with a two-edged knife, he cuts away the branches and the leaves of words, and nothing is left but the naked stalks of human life. The priests, and those of pompous show, rebuke the pruner, and would stop him in his work. But harvest time will come, and they who scorned the pruner will look again and be amazed! For they will see the human stalks, which seemed so lifeless, bending low with precious fruit. They will hear the harvesters rejoice, because the harvest is so great.'

The priests were unhappy with Jesus' words but they did not rebuke him, as they feared the multitude.

Vidyapati and the Hebrew sage often met, and talked about the needs of nations and of men, the sacred doctrines, and forms and rites best suited to the coming age. One day they sat together in a mountain pass, and Jesus said, 'The coming age will surely not require priests, shrines and the sacrifice of life. There is no power in the sacrifice of beast or bird to help a man to reach the holy life.'

Vidyapati replied, 'All forms and rites are symbols of what a man must do to attain the holy life, within the temple of the soul. The Holy One requires man to give his life in willing sacrifice for men, and all the offerings on altars and shrines, that have been made since time immemorial, were made to instruct man how to give himself to save his brother. Man can never save himself unless he loses his life to save another. The perfect age will not require forms, rites and carnal sacrifice. The coming age, however, is not the perfect age, and men will call for object lessons and symbolic rites. In the great religion you shall introduce to men some simple rites of washings and remembrances. But cruel sacrifices of animals, and birds, are not required by the gods.'

Jesus said, 'Our God must loathe the tinselled show of priests and priestly garbs. When men array themselves in ostentatious robes, to indicate that they are the servants of the gods, and strut about like gaudy peacocks, to be admired by men, because of their piety, the Holy One must turn away in sheer disgust! All people are equal and alike, the servants of our Father-God, and are themselves kings and priests. Will not the coming age demand complete destruction of the priestly caste, as well as every other caste and inequality amongst the sons of men?'

SECTION VII
The Life and Works of Jesus in Tibet and Western India

In Lhasa, Tibet, there was a master's temple, rich in manuscripts of ancient lore. The Indian sage had already read these manuscripts, and he revealed to Jesus many of the secret lessons they contained, but Jesus wished to study them for himself. Also, Meng-tzu, the greatest sage of the Far East, was in this Tibetan temple. The path across the Emodus Heights was very difficult, but Jesus started on his way, and Vidyapati gave him a trustworthy guide. Vidyapati sent a message to Meng-tzu, in which he told him about the young Hebrew sage, and asked for him to receive a welcome from the temple priests. After many days and great perils, the guide and Jesus reached the Lhasa Temple. Meng-tzu opened wide the temple doors, and all the priests and masters welcomed the young Hebrew sage.

They gave Jesus access to all their sacred manuscripts and, with the help of Meng-tzu, he read all of them. Meng-tzu often talked with Jesus about the coming age, and the sacred service best adapted for that generation. Jesus did not teach in Lhasa. When he had finished his studies, he travelled towards the west. On his way he stayed in different villages for a time and did teach. At last he reached the pass, and in the Ladakh city, Leh, he was favourably received by the monks, the merchants and the men of low estate. He stayed in the monastery and taught there. He sought the common people in the markets of trade and commerce, and taught there also. Nearby a woman lived, whose infant son was ill, and approaching death. The doctors had declared that there was no hope, and the child would surely die. The woman had heard that Jesus was a teacher sent by God, and she believed he had the power to heal her son. She clasped the dying infant in her arms and ran hastily to see that man of God. When Jesus recognized her faith, he lifted up his eyes to heaven and said, 'My Father-God, let your power divine overshadow me, and let the Holy Spirit fill this child that he may live!' Then in the presence of the crowds, he laid his hand upon the child and said, 'Good woman, you are indeed blest, your faith has saved your son.' Miraculously the child recovered, and was well again. The people were astonished and said, 'This surely must be the Holy One made flesh, for man alone cannot rebuke a sickness like this and save a child from death!' Then many of the people brought their sick, and Jesus spoke the Word, and they were healed.

Among the Ladakhs, Jesus stayed for many days. He taught them how to heal, how sins are blotted out, and how to make, on Earth, a heaven of joy. The people adored him for his words and deeds, and when he decided to leave, they grieved like children grieve when their mother departs. When he left that morning, the multitude was there to press his hand. Before leaving he addressed them with a parable.

'A certain king so loved the people of his land that he sent his only son to give precious gifts for all. The son went everywhere, scattering gifts lavishly all over the land. But there were priests who ministered at shrines of foreign gods, who were displeased, because the king had not dispensed the gifts through them. So they decided to stir up the people to hate the son, claiming that these gifts were worthless counterfeits. So the gullible people threw the precious gems, gold and silver, into the streets. They caught the son and beat him, spat on him and drove him away. The son did not resent their insults and treatment, but prayed instead, saying, "My Father-God, forgive these creatures of your hand, they are slaves, and know not what they do." And while they were still beating him, he handed out food and blessed them with his boundless love. In certain cities, the son was received with great joy, and he would have stayed to bless their homes, but he did not wait, as he wished to carry gifts to everyone in the whole of his father's kingdom.' Then Jesus said, 'My Father-God is King of all mankind, and He has sent me forth with all the bounties of His incomparable love and infinite wealth to all the peoples of all lands. I must bear these gifts, this living water and the bread of life! I go my way, but we shall meet again, for in my Fatherland there is room for all, and I shall prepare a place for you.' He raised his hands in silent benediction and went on his way.

A caravan of merchants was journeying through the Kashmir vale as Jesus passed that way, and they were going to Lahore, a city of the Hind, the five-stream land. These merchants had heard the prophet speak, had witnessed his mighty works in Leh, and they were very glad to meet him once more. When they heard that he was going to Lahore, and then across the Sind, through Persia and the farther west, and that he had no beast to ride, they gladly offered him a noble bactrian beast, well saddled and equipped, so he could journey with their caravan. When he reached Lahore, Ajainin and some other Brahmins priests greeted him with delight.

One day in Lahore, Ajainin sat with Jesus in the temple porch while a band of wandering singers and musicians paused before the court to sing and play. Their music was lively and tuneful. Jesus said that among the highly bred people of the land, he had heard no sweeter music than these uncouth children of the wilderness had brought here. From where had this power and talent come? In one short life they surely could not gain such grace of voice, and such knowledge of the laws of harmony and tone. Men call them prodigies, but there were no prodigies. Everything results from natural law. These people are not young. A thousand years would not suffice to give them such divine expressiveness, and such purity of voice and touch. Ten thousand years ago these people mastered harmony. In days of old they trod the busy thoroughfares of life, and caught the melody of birdsong, and played on harps of perfect form. Now they have come again to learn still other lessons from the varied notes of manifestations. These wandering peoples form a part of heaven's orchestra, and in the land of perfect things, the very angels will delight to hear them play and sing.

Then Jesus taught the common folk of Lahore. He healed their sick and showed them the way to rise to better lives by helpfulness to others. He said, 'We are not rich by what we get and hold. The only real things we keep are those we give away. If you would live the perfect life, give forth your life in service for your kind, and for forms of life that men will esteem the lower forms of life.'

But Jesus could not stay any longer in Lahore. He said farewell to the priests and other friends, and then took his camel and went his way towards Sind.

Here this Section ends. In the next Section he enters Persia. But as we are concerned with Jesus' visit to India and Tibet I will take up the story later, with his dramatic reappearance in India after the Crucifixion.

SECTION XXI
Chapter 176

Ravanna, Prince of India, gave a magnificent feast. He chose his palace in Orissa, the place where men of wisdom from the whole of the Far East were accustomed to meet. Ravanna was the same prince with whom the boy Jesus went to India many years before. The feast was held in honour of the wise sages of the East. Among the guests were Meng-tzu, Vidyapati and Lamaas. The wise men sat at table discussing the needs of India and the world in general. The door opening on to the banqueting hall was on the eastern side. There was a vacant chair at the table, also on the eastern side. As the wise men conversed a stranger entered, unannounced, and raising up his hands in benediction said, 'All hail!' A halo rested on his head, and a bright light, similar to sunlight, filled the hall. The wise men all rose spontaneously, bowed their heads and responded, 'All hail!'

Jesus sat down in the empty chair, and the wise men realized it was the Hebrew prophet who had come. Jesus said, 'Behold, for I am risen from the dead. Look at my hands, my feet, my side. The Roman soldiers pierced my hands and feet with nails, and then one pierced my heart. They put me in a tomb, and then I wrestled with death, the conqueror of men. I conquered Death, I stamped upon him and rose up. I brought immortality to light and painted on the walls of time a rainbow for the sons of men; and what I did all men shall do. This gospel of the resurrection of the dead is not only confined to Jew and Greek, it is the heritage of every man of every time and clime. And I am here as a demonstration of the power of man.' Then he arose and pressed the hand of every man and of his royal host, and said, 'Behold, I am not myth made of the fleeting winds, for I am flesh, bone and brawn, but I can cross the borderland at will.' Then they discussed together a long, long time. Then Jesus said, 'I go on my way, but you shall go to all the world and preach the gospel of the omnipotence of man, the power of truth, the resurrection of the dead. He who believes this gospel of the son of man shall never die, the dead shall live again.' Then Jesus disappeared, but he had sown the seed. The words of life were spoken in Orissa, and all of India heard.

This ends the Aquarian Gospel's accounts of Jesus in India and Tibet. After this Indian reappearance, Jesus appears again to the Magian priests in Persia, then in Israel, Greece, Rome, and finally to the Apostles. In this Chapter I shall not discuss the arguments for and against Dowling's revelation. I shall reserve that for the concluding chapter. Meanwhile we shall move on to Notovitch and the Gospel of Issa, which he discovered in Tibet.

Chapter 3

The Tibetan Gospel of Issa

Nicolai Alexandrovitch Notovitch, the celebrated adventurer, soldier, historian, diplomat, journalist, explorer, playwright, musician and author, was born in 1858 in the Crimea, the second son of a Jewish rabbi. Little is known about his early life, but he must have received a sound education in order to enter the University of St Petersburg where he studied history. Before attending the university, he had been conscripted and fought in the Serbian campaign against the Turks in 1876. He also took part in the Russian–Turkish War of 1877–8. He served with the Cossacks and was promoted to the rank of Officer.

He must have been a highly gifted young man to have been promoted to the rank of Officer in the elite Russian Cossacks. On release from military service in the 1880s, he wrote and produced two plays, *Ideal Marriage* and *Gallia*, for which he also composed the incidental music. Both plays achieved critical acclaim. He then found employment as a journalist and worked for a distinguished St Petersburg daily newspaper as Oriental correspondent. Because of the prevalence of anti-semitism in Russia at that time, he had converted to the Russian Orthodox Church. He wrote two books on the question of the proposed Russian–Franco Alliance. Then between 1883 and 1887, he was again an Oriental correspondent, but now for the renowned journal *Novaya Vremiya* and undertook a number of journeys, on their behalf, through the Balkans, the Caucasus, Central Asia and Persia. In 1887 he set out on his exploratory journey to India and Tibet. After this remarkable exploration he returned to Paris to write for the French press. It was in Paris that he handed in his sensational manuscript on the *Unknown Life of Jesus Christ* which was published in French in 1894. He was, however, arrested in Russia, while on a visit to St Petersburg in 1895, and accused of subversive literary activity which endangered the Orthodox Religion of the State. He was exiled without trial, because of insufficient evidence, to Siberia. There he continued to write articles on his travels which appeared in different French journals. In Siberia he also wrote a successful novel called *A Frenchman in Siberia: the Memoirs of a Russian Revolutionary*. He travelled to Egypt in 1898 and then on his return established a journal in Paris called *La Russie*, which mainly concerned itself with political and economic affairs along with his own articles. In 1899 he was accepted into the celebrated Societé d'Histoire Diplomatique. From 1903–6 he lived in London. His activities in England are not recorded, and there has been certain speculation that he may have been engaged in espionage for the French government. In 1906 there was an extensive contract drawn up between him and the Shah of Persia for the construction of roads and pipelines in Iran. In 1910 an edition of his notorious book on Jesus appeared in Russia under the title of *The Life of Saint Isa*. Up to 1916 he was editor and publisher of various periodicals in St Petersburg. After that there is no trace of the further career and activities of this talented and adventurous man.

It is with his discoveries about the unknown life of Jesus in India and Tibet that we are principally concerned. We know that in 1887 he reached Kashmir, on one of his many journeys as an Oriental correspondent, and then moved on to Ladakh in Tibet. He eventually arrived at a Buddhist monastery where he heard about the prophet Issa who had visited Tibet nearly 2,000 years ago. The memorable conversation with the head lama is recorded by Notovitch as follows:

Lama: 'The only difference between the Christians and ourselves is that, after having adopted the great doctrines of Buddha, the Christians have parted from him completely by creating for themselves a different Dalai Lama. Our Dalai Lama alone retained the divine gift of seeing the majesty of Buddha, and the power to act as an intermediary between Earth and Heaven.'

Notovitch: 'Who is this Christian Dalai Lama you are talking about? We have a Son of God to whom we direct our fervent prayers and whom in time of need we beseech to intercede for us with our one and indivisible God ...'

Lama: 'It is not of him I speak, Sahib! We too respect the one you recognize as Son of the One God, not that we see in him an only Son, rather a Being perfect among all the elect. The spirit of Buddha was indeed incarnate in the sacred person of Issa who, without aid from fire or sword, has spread knowledge of our great and true religion throughout the world. I speak instead of your earthly Dalai Lama, him to whom you have given the title "Father of the Church". This is a great sin; may the flocks be forgiven who have gone astray because of it …'

Notovitch: (understood the Lama was probably referring to the Pope) 'You tell me that a son of Buddha, Issa, spread your religion over the Earth. Who is he then?'

Lama: 'Issa is a great prophet, one of the first after the twenty-two Buddhas. He is greater than any one of the Dalai Lamas, for he constitutes part of the spiritual essence of our Lord. It is he who has enlightened you, who has brought back within the fold of religion the souls of the erring, and allows every human being to distinguish between good and evil. His name and his deeds are recorded in our secret writings.'

This conversation led Notovitch to investigate more about Issa and to search for the manuscript containing his teaching. He felt that the name Issa was certainly a Tibetan alliteration for the name Jesus, or more probably the Hebrew Jeshua, and he was determined to find out more. The name of Moses was similarly translated as Mossa. Further enquiries in Lhasa led him to the Hemis Monastery where he was told that in their large collection, the manuscript may well be found. There he did indeed find the Gospel of Issa, and it was read to him by a Tibetan translator. The text is again in neo-biblical phraseology, and the following is an extract from the Foreword by Notovitch, then all 14 chapters, broken down into verses, which I will paraphrase into contemporary English. Without reading the whole of the Gospel of Issa, it is impossible for us to form a judgement on the veracity and authenticity of the text. This gospel was included in Notovitch's sensational *Unknown Life of Jesus*, his own transcription from his Pali translator, from which the reverberations are still echoing today. Its interpretation of the Exodus from Egypt is novel, to say the least.

THE LIFE OF SAINT ISSA
Best of the Sons of Men
An Extract from Nicolai Notovitch's Foreword

After the close of the Turko–Russian War (1877–8) I undertook a series of extended journeys through the Far East. Having visited all points of interest in the Balkans, I crossed the Caucasian Mountains into Central Asia and Persia, and finally in 1879, made an excursion into India.

The first object of this journey was to study the customs and habits of the inhabitants of India in their own surroundings, as well as to study the grand, mysterious archaeology and the colossal, majestic nature of the country. Wandering without any settled course from one locality to another, I finally came to mountainous Afghanistan, whence I reached India through the picturesque passes of Bolan and Guernai. I then followed the Indus to Rawalpindi, travelled through the Punjab – the country of five rivers – visited the golden temple of Amritsar, near Lahore, and proceeded towards Kashmir, the 'vale of eternal happiness'. There I began my wanderings as fancy or curiosity guided or dictated until I reached Ladakh, where I intended to make a somewhat lengthy stay before returning to Russia through eastern Turkestan and Karakorum.

In the course of one of my visits to a Buddhist convent, I learned from the chief lama that there existed very ancient memoirs, treating of the life of Christ and the nations of the Far East, in the archives of Lhasa, and that a few of the larger monasteries possessed copies and translations of these precious chronicles.

There being little probability of my early return to Tibet, I resolved to delay my return to Europe, and verify these assertions by seeing some of these copies, even though I was obliged to invade every convent as far as Lhasa – a journey far less perilous and difficult to accomplish than we are usually led to believe. Besides this I was so well accustomed to the dangers encountered by the traveller in those regions that they no longer harboured any terrors for me.

During my sojourn in Leh, the capital of Ladakh, I visited Hemis, a large convent in the outskirts of the city, where I was informed by the lama that the monastic libraries contained a few copies of the manuscript in question.

That I might not arouse the suspicions of the authorities in regard to the object of my visit to the convent, and raise no obstacles to a subsequent journey into Tibet – as a Russian – on my return to Leh I announced my immediate departure for India, and again left the capital of Ladakh.

An unfortunate accident, whereby my leg was injured, gave me an unexpected excuse to enter the monastery, where I received excellent care and nursing; and I took advantage of my short stay among these monks to obtain the privilege of seeing the manuscripts relating to Christ. With the aid of my interpreter, who translated from the Tibetan, I carefully transcribed the verses as they were read by the Lama.

I entertained no doubt whatsoever of the authenticity of this narrative, written with the utmost precision by Brahmin historians and Buddhists from India and Nepal. My intention was made to publish the translation on my return to Europe.

CHAPTER 1

The earth has trembled and the heavens have wept because of a great crime committed in the land of Israel. They have tortured there, and put to death, the great and just Issa, in whom dwelt the soul of the universe, incarnate in a simple mortal, in order to do good to men and exterminate their evil thoughts. And bring back man, degraded by his sins, to a life of peace, love and happiness. And to recall to him the One and indivisible Creator, whose mercy is infinite and without bounds. Listen to what the merchants from Israel relate to us on this subject.

CHAPTER 2

The people of Israel, who dwelt on fertile soil, giving forth two crops a year, and who possessed large flocks, incited by their sins the anger of God. He inflicted upon them a terrible chastisement in taking from them their land, their cattle and their possessions. Israel was reduced to slavery by the powerful and rich Pharaohs who reigned in Egypt. They treated the Israelites worse than animals, burdening them with onerous tasks and binding them in chains. They covered their bodies with weals and wounds, without giving them sufficient food or permitting them to dwell beneath a roof. They kept them in a state of continual terror to deprive them of all human resemblance. In their great calamity, the people of Israel remembered their heavenly protector and praying to Him, implored His grace and mercy.

An illustrious Pharaoh then reigned in Egypt; he had rendered himself famous by his numerous victories, the riches he had accumulated, and the vast palaces which his slaves had erected for him with their own hands. This Pharaoh had two sons, of whom the younger was called Mossa. Learned Israelites taught him many diverse sciences. They loved Mossa in Egypt, for his goodness and the compassion which he showed to all those who suffered. Seeing that the Israelites would not, in spite of the intolerable sufferings they were enduring, abandon their God to worship those made by the hand of man, which were the gods of the Egyptian nation, Mossa believed in their invisible God who would not allow their failing strength to give way. The Israelite elders aroused the concern of Mossa, and had recourse to him, praying that he would intercede with Pharaoh, his father, in favour of their people. So Prince Mossa went to his father, begging him to ameliorate the fate of these unfortunate slaves. But Pharaoh was angered by his request, and consequentially increased the torments endured by his slaves. It happened after a short time that a great evil visited Egypt. A pestilence came to decimate the young, the old, the weak and the strong. The Pharaoh believed in the resentment of his own gods towards him. But Prince Mossa told his father that it was the God of his slaves who was interceding in favour of these unfortunates in punishing the Egyptians. The Pharaoh then gave his son Mossa an order to take all the slaves of the Hebrew race, and conduct them out of the city, and to found at a great distance from the capital another city where he should live amongst them. Mossa then informed the Hebrew slaves that he had set them free in the name of their God, the God of Israel, and he led them from the city and the land of Egypt. He took them into the land they had lost by their many sins, he gave them laws, and commanded them to always pray to the invisible Creator whose goodness is infinite. On the death of Prince Mossa, the Israelites strictly obeyed his laws, whereby their God recompensed them for the ills to which He had exposed them in Egypt. Their kingdom became the most powerful in all the Earth, their kings made themselves famous for their treasures, and a long period of peace reigned among the people of Israel.

CHAPTER 3

The glory of Israel's riches spread throughout the world, and the neighbouring nations were envious. For the Most High, Himself, led the victorious arms of the Hebrews, and the pagans dared not attack them. Unhappily, as man is not always true to himself, the fidelity of the Israelites to their God did not last long. They began by forgetting all the favours which He had heaped upon them, seldom invoked His name, and sought the protection of magicians and sorcerers. The kings and captains substituted their own laws for those which Mossa had written down for them. The temple of God and the practice of worship were abandoned. The people gave themselves up to pleasure and lost their original purity. Several centuries had elapsed since their departure from Egypt when God determined to exercise once more His chastisements upon them. Strangers began to invade the land of Israel, devastating the country, ruining the villages, and carrying the inhabitants into captivity. At one time, there came pagans from the country of Romeles, on the other side of the sea. They subdued the Hebrews, and established among them military leaders who, delegated by their Caesar, ruled over them. They destroyed the temples and forced the inhabitants to cease worshipping their invisible God, and compelled them to sacrifice victims to pagan deities. They made warriors of those who had been nobles, the women were torn away from their husbands, and the lower classes, reduced to slavery, were sent by thousands beyond the seas. As to their children, they were put to the sword. Soon, in the whole land of Israel, nothing was heard but groans and lamentations. In their extreme distress, the people remembered their Almighty God. They implored Him for His Grace, and begged Him to forgive them. Our Father, in His inexhaustible mercy, heard their prayer.

CHAPTER 4

At this time came the moment when the All-Merciful Judge elected to become incarnate in a human being. The Eternal Spirit, dwelling in a state of complete inaction and of supreme beatitude, awoke and detached itself, for an indefinite period, from the Eternal Being, so as to demonstrate, in the guise of humanity, the means of self-identification with Divinity, and of attaining eternal felicity. Also, to show by example how man may attain moral purity, and by separating his soul from its mortal coil, the degree of perfection necessary to enter into the Kingdom of Heaven, which is immutable, and where happiness reigns eternally.

Soon afterwards, a marvellous child was born in the land of Israel, God Himself speaking through the mouth of this infant, about the body's frailty and the soul's grandeur. The parents of the new-born child were poor people, belonging by birth to a family of noted piety, who forgetting their ancient splendour on Earth, praised the name of the Creator, and thanked Him for the troubles by which He saw fit to prove them. To reward them for not turning aside from the way of truth, God blessed the first-born of this family. He chose their son as His Elect, and sent him to help those who had fallen into evil ways, and to cure those who suffered.

This divine child, to whom was given the name of Issa, began from his earliest years to speak of the One and indivisible God, exhorting the souls of those who had gone astray to repentance and the purification of the sins of which they were culpable.

People flocked from all parts of Israel to hear him, and

they marvelled at the discourses proceeding from his childish mouth. All the Israelites were of one accord in saying that the Eternal Spirit dwelt in this child. When Issa had attained the age of 13 years, the time when an Israelite entered manhood, and could take a wife, the house where his parents earned a livelihood by carrying on a modest trade began to be a place for rich and noble people, desiring of having for a son-in-law, the young Issa, already famous for his edifying discourses in the name of the Almighty. Then it was that Issa left his parental home in secret, departed from Jerusalem, and with some merchants set out towards Sind, with the aim of perfecting himself in the Divine Word and of studying the laws of the Great Buddhas.

CHAPTER 5

When he was 14, the young Issa, blessed of God, came this side of the Sind, and established himself among the Aryas in the land beloved of God. Fame spread the reputation of this marvellous child throughout the length of northern Sind, and when he crossed the country of the five rivers and the Rajputana, the devotees of the god Jaine prayed for him to live among them. But he left the erring worshippers of Jaine and went to Juggernaut in the land of Orissa, where the mortal remains of Vyasa-Krishna remain; and where the white priests of Brahman made him a joyous welcome. They taught him to read and understand the Vedas, to cure by aid of prayer, to teach, to explain the holy scriptures to the people, and to drive out evil spirits from the bodies of men, restoring them back to sanity.

He spent six years at Juggernaut, at Rajagriha, at Benares, and in the other holy cities. Everyone loved him, for Issa lived in peace with the merchants and the untouchables whom he instructed in the holy scriptures. But the Brahmins and the warrior class told him that they were forbidden by the great Parabrahman to come near to those whom he had created from his side and feet, and that the merchants were permitted to hear the reading of the Vedas only on festival days. Also that the untouchables were forbidden not only to assist at the reading of the Vedas, but also from contemplating them, for their condition was to serve in perpetuity as slaves to the Brahmins, the warrior class and even the merchants. 'Only death can set them free from their servitude, as Parabrahman has said. Leave them, and then come to worship with us the gods, who will become incensed against you, if you disobey them.'

But Issa did not pay attention to their discourses, but took himself to the untouchables, preaching against the priests of the Brahmin and warrior class. He spoke out strongly against the acts of men granting themselves the power to deprive their fellow beings of their human rights. 'For,' said he, 'God the Father makes no distinction between any of His children. All to Him are equally dear.' Issa denied the divine origin of the Vedas and the Puranas, 'For,' he taught his followers, 'a law has already been given to man to guide him in his actions, fear thy God, bend the knee before Him only, and bring to Him alone the offerings which proceed from your gains.' Issa denied the Trimurti, and the incarnation of Parabrahman in Vishnu, Siva, and other gods, for he said, 'The Judge Eternal, the Eternal Spirit, comprehends the one and indivisible soul of the universe, which alone creates, contains and vivifies all. He alone has willed and created, He alone has existed since all eternity, and His existence will have no end. He has no equal either in the heavens or on Earth. The Great Creator has not shared his power with any living being, still less with inanimate objects, as they have taught to you; for He alone possesses omnipotence. He willed it and the world appeared. In a divine thought, He gathered together the waters, separating them from the dry portions of the globe. He is the principle of the mysterious existence of man, in whom He has breathed a part of His Being. He has subordinated to man the earth, the waters, the beasts and all that He has created. He preserves all that in immutable order, fixing for each thing the length of its duration. The wrath of God will soon be let loose against man, for he has forgotten his Creator, he has filled his temples with abominations, and he worships a host of creatures which God has made subordinate to him. For to honour stones and metals, he sacrifices human beings, in whom dwells a part of the spirit of the Most High. For he humiliates those who work by the sweat of their brow to acquire the favour of an idler seated at his sumptuous board. Those who deprive their brethren of divine happiness shall be deprived of it themselves. The Brahmins and the warrior class shall become the untouchables, and with the untouchables the Eternal shall dwell eternally. Because on the Day of the Last Judgement, the untouchables and the merchants will be forgiven much, because of their ignorance. But God, on the contrary, will punish with His wrath those who have arrogated to themselves His rights!'

The merchants and the untouchables were filled with great admiration and asked Issa how they should pray so as not to lose their eternal felicity.

'Do not worship idols, for they will not hear you. Do not listen to the Vedas, their truth is false. Never put yourself in the first place, never humiliate your neighbour. Help the poor, support the weak, do ill to no one, and do not covet that which you have not, and which you see as belonging to another.'

CHAPTER 6

The Brahmin priests and the warriors, becoming acquainted with Issa's discourses addressed to the untouchables, resolved upon his death and sent with murderous intent their servants to seek out the young prophet. Issa, however, was warned of this threat by some untouchables, and left the Juggernaut neighbourhood by night, establishing himself in the country of Gautamides, birthplace of the Great Buddha Sakyamuni, in the midst of a people worshipping the One and only Brahman.

After perfecting himself in Pali, the just Issa applied himself to the study of the sacred writings of the sutras. Six years afterwards, Issa, whom the Buddha had chosen to spread his holy word, had become a perfect expositor of the sacred writings. Then he left Nepal and the Himalayas, descended into the Rajputana valley and travelled westwards, preaching to diverse peoples the supreme perfection of man. That is, to do good towards one's neighbour, that being a sure means of merging oneself rapidly in the Eternal Spirit. 'He who shall have regained his original purity,' said Issa, 'will die having obtained remission for his sins, and he will have the right to contemplate the majesty of God!'

In crossing pagan lands, the divine Issa taught that the worship of idols was contrary to the law of nature. 'For man,' said he, 'has not been permitted to see the image of God, and yet he has fashioned a host of deities in the likeness of the Eternal. Moreover, it is incompatible with the human conscience to give a place of lesser importance to the grandeur of divine creation in the animal kingdom, than to objects executed by the hand of man in stone or metal. The Eternal lawgiver is One, there is no other God than He! He has not shared His creation with anyone, nor has He informed anyone of His intentions. Even as a father would act towards his children, so shall God judge men after their death, according to the laws of His mercy. Never would He so humiliate His child as to transmigrate his soul, as in a purgatory, into an animal body!'

'The heavenly law,' said the Creator through the mouth of Issa, 'is opposed to the immolation of human sacrifices to an image or to an animal; for I have consecrated for man, all the animals and all that the Earth contains. All things have been sacrificed to man, who is directly and intimately associated with me his Father; therefore he who shall have stolen His child from Him, will be severely judged and chastised by the divine law. Man is nothing before the Eternal Judge, as the animal is nothing before man. Therefore I say, leave your idols and do not perform rites which separate you from your Father, by associating with those priests from whom the heavens have turned away. For it is they who have led you from the true God, and whose superstitions and cruelties lead to your soul's perversion and the loss of your moral sense.'

CHAPTER 7

The words of Issa spread among the pagans in all the countries he visited. The priests asked Issa, who glorified the name of the true God, to give good reason, in the presence of the people, why he made reproaches against them, and ridiculed the nullity of their idols? Issa answered them and said, 'If your idols and your animals are so powerful, and really possess supernatural strength, then let them strike me to the ground!'

'Work then a miracle!' the priests responded, 'and let thy God confound our Gods, if they inspire Him with contempt!'

Issa replied, 'The miracles of my God have been worked since the very first day when the universe was created! Furthermore, they take place every day and every moment. Whoever does not see them is deprived of one of the greatest gifts of life! And it is not only against pieces of stone, metal or wood, which are inanimate, that the anger of God will have full force; but it will fall on those men who, if they desire salvation, have not destroyed all the idols they have made. Even as a stone and a grain of sand, nothing as they are in the sight of men, wait patiently for the moment when he shall take and make use of them, so man, too, must await the great favour that God shall accord him in His final judgement. So woe unto you, enemies of men, it isn't His grace you await, but rather His wrath. Woe unto you, if you expect miracles to bear witness to His power! For it will not be the idols that He will annihilate in His anger, but those who shall have erected them. Their hearts will be consumed with eternal fire, and their lacerated bodies will go to satisfy the hunger of wild beasts. God will drive the impure from His flock, but will take back unto to Himself those who have gone astray through not having recognized the portion of His spirit that lies within them.'

Seeing the powerlessness of their priests, the pagans had still greater faith in the sayings of Issa and, fearing the anger of his Divinity, broke their idols to pieces. As for the priests, they fled to escape the vengeance of the populace. Issa further taught the pagans not to strive to see the Eternal Spirit just with their eyes, but to endeavour to feel Him in their hearts, and by purity of soul to render themselves worthy of His grace.

He said to them, 'Not only abstain from consuming animal sacrifices, but immolate no creature to whom life has been given, for everything that exists has been created for the benefit of mankind. Do not steal the goods of your neighbour, for that would deprive him of what he has acquired by the sweat of his brow. Deceive no one, so as not to be deceived yourselves. Endeavour to justify yourself before the last judgement, for then it will be too late. Do not give yourself up to debauchery, for that would be to violate God's laws. You shall attain supreme happiness, not only in purifying yourselves, but also in guiding others in the way that shall permit them to gain original perfection!'

CHAPTER 8

The neighbouring countries resounded with the prophecies of Issa, and when he entered into Persia the priests became alarmed and forbade the inhabitants to listen to him. But when they saw all the villagers welcoming him with joy and listening devoutly to his sermons, they gave orders to arrest him and had him brought before the high priest where he underwent the following interrogation.

'Of what new God are you speaking? Are you unaware, unhappy man, that Saint Zoroaster is the only just one allowed the privilege of communion with the Supreme Being? He commanded the angels to write down the word of God for the use of his people, laws that were given to Zoroaster in paradise. Who are you to dare blaspheme our God and to sow doubts in the hearts of believers?'

Issa replied, 'It is not about some new god that I speak, but of our Heavenly Father, who has existed since all time, and who will still exist after the end of all worlds. It is of Him that I have told the people, who like innocent children are incapable of comprehending God by the simple strength of their intelligence; or of penetrating into His divine and spiritual sublimity. But even as a babe discovers its mother's breast in the darkness, so even your people, who have been led into error by your false doctrines and ceremonies, have recognized by their instinct their Father of whom I am the prophet. The Eternal Being has said to your people through my utterances that you should not worship the Sun, for it is only a part of the world which I have created for man. The Sun rises in order to warm you while you work, it sets to all of you the rest which I myself have appointed. It is to I and

I alone that you owe all that you possess, all that is to be found about, above and below!'

'But,' said the priests, 'how can a people live according to the laws of justice without rulers?' Issa replied, 'So long as the people were without priests, the natural law governed them, and they preserved the honesty of their souls. Their souls were with God, and to commune with their Father they did not need the intermediary of an idol or animal, nor of fire, as it is practised here. You contend that one must worship the Sun, the spirits of good and evil. Well, I say to you that your doctrines are false. The Sun does not act independently, but according to the will of the invisible Creator who gave it birth; and has willed it to be the star that lights the day, and to warm the body of the labourer and the seed which he sows. God is like a Father of a family and only does good to His children, forgiving all their faults if they repent. The spirit of evil dwells on Earth in the hearts of men who turn aside the children of God from the straight path. So I say to you, beware of the day of judgement of God, for He will inflict a terrible chastisement upon all those who have led His children astray from the straight path, and have filled them with superstition and prejudice. If you blind those that can see, you convey contagion to the healthy, and teach the worship of things that God has subordinated to man for his good, and to aid him in his work. Your doctrine is the fruit of your errors, for desiring to bring nearer to you the God of truth, you have created for yourselves false gods.'

After listening to him the Magi decided not to harm him. But that night, when the town lay sleeping, they took him outside their walls, and left him on the high road, in the hope he would soon become prey to wild beasts. But protected by the Lord our God, Saint Issa journeyed on his way unmolested.

CHAPTER 9

Issa, whom the Creator had chosen to remind a depraved humanity of their true God, had reached the age of 29 when he returned to the land of Israel. Since his departure the heathen had inflicted even more atrocious sufferings on the Israelites, who were prey to deepest despondency. Many among them had begun to abandon the laws of their God and those of Mossa in the hope of appeasing their savage conquerors. In the face of this evil, Issa exhorted his compatriots not to despair, because the day of redemption from their sins was at hand. He confirmed them in the faith which they had in the God of their fathers.

He said, 'Children, do not give yourselves up to despondency, for your Heavenly Father has heard your voice and your cries have reached Him. Do not weep, my beloved ones! For your grief has touched your Father's heart, and He has forgiven you, even as He forgave your ancestors. Do not allow your families to fall into debauchery or lose their noble feelings. Do not worship idols who are deaf to your voices. Fill my temple with your hope and your patience, and do not forsake the religion of your fathers, for I alone have guided them, and heaped benefits upon them. You shall raise up those who have fallen, you shall give food to the hungry, you shall aid the sick, so as to be wholly pure and just at the day of the last judgement which I prepare for you.'

The Israelites flocked to hear the words of Issa, asking him where they should praise the Heavenly Father; seeing that the enemy had razed their temples to the ground and laid low their sacred vessels. Issa answered them by saying that God had not in view temples erected by men's hands, for the human heart was the true temple of God.

He said, 'Enter into the temple of your heart. Illumine it with good thoughts, the patience and the immovable faith which you should have in your Father. Your sacred vessels are your hands and eyes. See and do that which is agreeable to God, for in doing good to your neighbour, you accomplish a rite which embellishes the temple wherein dwells He who gave you life. For God has created you in His own image – innocent, with pure souls and hearts filled with goodness, not destined for the conception of evil schemes, but made to be sanctuaries of love and justice. Therefore do not stain your hearts, for the Supreme Being dwells there eternally. If you wish to accomplish works marked with love or piety, perform them with an open heart and do not let your deeds be governed by calculations or the hope of gain. For such actions will not help you to reach your salvation, and you will fall into that state of moral degradation where theft, lying and murder pass for generous deeds!'

CHAPTER 10

Saint Issa went from one town to another, strengthening through the word of God the courage of the Israelites, who were ready to succumb to the weight of their despair.

Thousands followed him to hear him preach. Soon the chiefs of the towns became afraid of him, and they informed the principal governor who lived in Jerusalem that a man named Issa had arrived in the country, and was stirring up the people, by his discourses against the authorities. Furthermore that the crowds listened to him with attention, neglected their duties to the state and prophesied that before long they would be rid of their intrusive rulers. Then Pilate, Governor of Jerusalem, ordered they should seize Issa, bring him into town and take him before the judges. However, so as not to excite the anger of the populace, Pilate charged the priests and the learned Hebrew elders to judge Issa in the Temple.

Meanwhile Issa, continuing his preaching, arrived at Jerusalem. Having learned of his arrival, all the inhabitants, knowing him already by reputation, went out to meet him. They greeted him respectfully and opened up the Temple gates in order to hear what he had preached in the other cities of Israel.

Issa addressed them and said, 'The human race perishes because of its lack of faith, for the darkness and tempest have scattered the flocks of humanity, and they have lost their shepherds. But the tempest will not last forever, and the darkness will not always obscure the light. The sky will become serene again, and the heavenly light will spread itself over all the Earth, and the flocks led astray will gather around their shepherd. Do not strive to find straight paths in the darkness, or you will fall into a pit, but gather together your remaining strength, support one another, place your faith in God, and wait until light appears. He who sustains his neighbour sustains himself; and whosoever protects his family, protects the people and the state. For be certain that the day is at hand when you shall be delivered from the darkness. You shall be gathered together as one family, and your enemy, who ignores the grace of God, shall tremble with fear!'

The priests and the elders who were listening to him were filled with admiration at his discourse; they asked him if it were true that he had tried to stir up the people against the country's authorities, as had been reported to Pilate? He answered, 'Can one incite to insurrection men gone astray, from whom obscuration has hidden their doorway and their path? I have only warned the unfortunate, as I do here in this Temple, so that they do not further advance along the darkened way, for an abyss is open under their feet. Earthly power is short and is subject to many changes. What use is it for man to revolt against it, seeing that one power always succeeds another? So it will always be until the end of humanity. But see that the mighty and rich do not sow, among the children of Israel, a spirit of rebellion against the eternal power of heaven!'

The elders then asked, 'Who are you, and from what country do you come? We have not heard of you before and we do not even know your name.' Issa replied, 'I am an Israelite. From the day of my birth I saw the walls of Jerusalem, and I heard the weeping of my brothers reduced to slavery, and the lamentations of my sisters who were carried away by the heathen. My soul was filled with sadness, when I saw that my brethren had forgotten the true God. As a child, I left my father's house and went to dwell among other peoples. But having heard that my brethren were suffering still greater torments, I have returned to the country where my parents dwell to remind my brothers of the faith of their forefathers, which teaches us patience on Earth to obtain perfect and sublime happiness in heaven.'

Then the elders questioned him further. 'It is said that you deny the laws of Mossa and that you teach the people to forsake God's temple.' Issa replied, 'One cannot demolish that which has been given by our Heavenly Father, in spite of all that has been destroyed by sinners, for I have urged the purification of one's heart from all blemish, for it is the true temple of God. As to the laws of Mossa, I have endeavoured to establish them in men's hearts. I say unto you that you do not understand their true meaning, for it is not vengeance, but mercy, that they teach. The spirit of these laws has been perverted!'

CHAPTER 11

Having listened to Issa, the priests and the elders decided not to judge him, as he harmed no one. So presenting themselves before Pilate, they addressed him in the following manner. 'We have seen the man whom you accuse of inciting our people to rebellion. We have heard his discourses, and we know him to be our compatriot. The chiefs of the cities have given you false reports, for he is a just man who teaches the people the word of God. After having interrogated him, we dismissed him, that he might go in peace.'

Pilate became angry and sent spies in disguise to watch Issa and all his actions, and report to the authorities the least word that he should address to the people.

Meanwhile Saint Issa continued to visit the neighbouring towns, preaching the true ways of the Creator, exhorting the Hebrews to patience, and promising them a speedy deliverance. During all this time, many people followed him, wherever he went, several never leaving him but becoming his disciples.

Issa said, 'Do not believe in miracles wrought by the hand of man, for He who dominates over nature is alone capable of doing that which is supernatural, whilst man is powerless to stay the angers of the winds or to spread the rain. Nevertheless, there is one miracle which it is possible for man to accomplish. It is when, full of a sincere belief, he decides to root out from his heart all evil thoughts, and when to attain this end he forsakes the paths of iniquity. For all things that are done without God are but errors, seductions and enchantments, which only demonstrate to what an extent the soul of him who practises this art is full of shamelessness, falsehood and impurity. Do not put your faith in oracles. God alone knows the future. He who has recourse to divination and diviners profanes the temple which is in his heart and gives a proof of distrust towards his Creator. Faith in diviners and their oracles destroys the innate simplicity of man and his child-like purity. An infernal power takes possession of him, forcing him to commit all kinds of crimes and to worship idols. Whereas the Lord our God, who has no equal, is One, all-mighty, omniscient and omnipresent. It is He who possesses all wisdom and all light. It is to Him that you must address yourselves to be consoled in your sorrows, helped in your works, and cured in your sickness. Whosoever shall have recourse to Him shall not be denied. The secret of nature is in the hands of God. For the world, before it appeared, existed in the depths of divine thought; it became material and visible by the will of the Most High. When you address yourselves to Him, become again as children; for you know not the past, nor the present, nor the future, and God is the Master of all time!'

CHAPTER 12

'Righteous man,' the spies sent by Pilate said to him, 'tell us if we shall perform the will of our Caesar or await our speedy deliverance?'

Issa, having recognized them as people sent to follow him, replied, 'I have not said to you that you shall be delivered from Caesar. It is the soul plunged in error that shall have its deliverance. As there can be no family without a head, so there can be no order among a people without a Caesar. Implicit obedience should be given to him, he alone being answerable for his acts before the supreme tribunal.'

'Does Caesar possess the divine right to rule?' asked one of the spies. 'And is he the best of mortals?'

'There should be no better among men, but there are also sufferers, whom those elected and charged with his mission should care for, making use of the means conferred on them by the sacred law of our heavenly Father. Mercy and justice are the highest attributes of a Caesar. His name will be illustrious if he adheres to them. But he who acts otherwise, who exceeds the limit of power that he has over his subordinates, going so far as to put their lives in danger, offends the Great Judge and loses his dignity in the sight of man.'

At this juncture, an old woman who had approached the group to hear Issa better was pushed aside by one of the spies, who placed himself in front of her. Then Issa said, 'It is not right that a son should set aside his mother, taking her place. Whoever does not respect his mother, the most sacred being after God, is unworthy of the name of son. Listen to what I am saying to you. Respect woman, for she is the mother of the universe, and all the truth of divine creation lies in her. She is the basis of all that is good and beautiful, as she is also the germ of life and death. On her depends the whole existence of man, for she is his natural and moral support. She gives birth to you in the midst of suffering. By the sweat of her brow she rears you, and until her death you cause her the gravest anxieties. Bless her and worship her, for she is your one friend, your one support on Earth. Respect her, and uphold her. In acting so, you will win her love and her heart. You will find favour in the sight of God and many sins shall be forgiven you. In the same way, love your wives and respect them, for they will be mothers tomorrow, and each, later, will be the ancestress of a family. Be lenient towards woman. Her love ennobles man, softens his heart, tames the brute in him, and makes of him a lamb. The wife and mother are the inappreciable treasures given to you by God. They are the fairest ornaments of existence, and by them shall be born all the world's inhabitants. Even as the God of battle of old separated the light from the darkness, the land from the waters, woman possesses the divine faculty of separating in a man good intentions from evil thoughts. Therefore, after God, your best thoughts should belong to the women and the wives, women being for you the temple wherein you will obtain the most easily perfect happiness. Imbue yourselves in this temple with moral strength! Here you will forget your sorrows and your failures. You will recover the lost energy necessary to enable you to help your neighbour. Do not expose her to humiliation. In acting so, you will humiliate yourselves and lose the sentiment of love, without which nothing exists here below. Protect your wife, so as she may protect you and all your family. All that you do for your wife, your mother, for a widow, or another woman in distress, you will have done unto your God!'

CHAPTER 13

Saint Issa taught the people in this way for three years, in every town and village; by the waysides and on the plains. All that he had predicted came to pass. During all this time, the disguised servants of Pilate watched him closely without hearing anything said like the reports made against Issa in former years by the chiefs of the towns. But the Governor Pilate, becoming alarmed at the very great popularity of Saint Issa, who according to his adversaries sought to stir up the people to proclaim him king, ordered one of his spies to accuse him. Then soldiers were commanded to proceed to his arrest, and they imprisoned him in a subterranean cell, where they tortured him to make a confession which would permit him to being sentenced to death.

The saint, thinking only of the perfect beatitude of his

brethren, bore all his sufferings in the name of his Creator. The servants of Pilate continued to torture him, and reduced him to a state of extreme weakness; but God was with him and did not allow him to die. Learning of the sufferings and the tortures which their saint was enduring, the high priests and the wise elders went to petition the governor to release Issa, in honour of an approaching festival. Pilate refused their request. They then asked him to permit Issa to appear before the Tribunal of the Ancients so that he might be condemned or acquitted before the festival. This request Pilate granted. The next day he assembled together the chief captains, priests, elders and lawyers, that they might judge Issa. They took him from his prison and seated him before the governor and two thieves, to be judged at the same time, in order to show the crowd that he was not the only one to be accused.

Pilate addressed Issa saying, 'Oh man, is it true that you incite the people against the authorities with the intention of becoming King of Israel?'

Issa replied, 'One does not become king at one's own will. Those who have told you that I stir up rebellion lie! I have never spoken other than about the King of Heaven, and it is He that I teach the people to worship. For the children of Israel have lost their original purity, and if they do not pay obeisance to their true God, they will be sacrificed, and their temple will fall into ruins. As the temporal power maintains order in a country, I teach them not to forget that law. I tell them to live in conformity with your station and your fortune, so as not to disturb public order. I have exhorted them also to remember that disorder reigns in their hearts and in their minds. Consequentially, the King of Heaven has punished them and suppressed their national kings. Nevertheless, I have told them that if they become resigned to their destinies, as a reward, the Kingdom of Heaven will be reserved for them.'

Then witnesses were brought forward, one of whom said, 'You have told the people that the temporal power is as naught compared to that King who will soon deliver the Israelites from the heathen yoke.'

'Blessed are you', said Issa, 'for having spoken truth. The King of Heaven is far greater and more powerful than the earthly law, and his Kingdom surpasses all the kingdoms of the Earth. The time is not far off when, conforming to the divine will, the people of Israel will purify themselves from their sins. For it has been prophesied that a forerunner will come to proclaim the deliverance of the people, gathering them into one fold.'

Then Pilate, addressing the court said, 'Do you hear? He confesses to the crime of which he is accused. Judge him, according to your laws, and sentence him to death.'

'We cannot condemn him', replied the priests and elders. 'You have just heard that his references were made according to the King of Heaven, and that he preached nothing to the children of Israel which constitutes an offence against our law.'

Pilate then sent for a witness who, at his instigation, would betray Issa. The man came and said to Issa, 'Didn't you pass yourself off as the King of Israel when you said that He who reigns in the heavens had sent you to prepare the people?'

Issa blessed him and said, 'You will be pardoned, for what you say does not come from yourself.'

Then addressing Pilate, he said, 'Why humiliate your dignity, and why teach your inferiors to live in falsehood, as by doing so, you condemn the innocent.'

At these words Pilate became angry and proclaimed the death sentence to be passed upon Issa, and the acquittal of the two thieves. The court, having consulted each other, said to Pilate, 'We cannot take upon our heads the great sin of condemning an innocent man and acquitting thieves. That would be against our law. Do as you will.' Saying which the priests and the elders left, washing their hands in a sacred vessel, saying, 'We are innocent of the death of this just man.'

CHAPTER 14

By the order of the governor, the soldiers seized Issa, and the two thieves, who they led to the place of execution, where they nailed them to crosses. All day the bodies remained suspended, terrible to see, under the guard of the soldiers. The people standing all around with the relations of the sufferers were praying and weeping. At sunset the sufferings of Issa were over. He lost consciousness, and the soul of this just man left his body to become absorbed in the Divinity.

So ended the earthly existence of the reflection of the Eternal Spirit, in the form of a man, who had saved hardened sinners and endured many sufferings.

Meanwhile Pontius Pilate became afraid of his deed, and gave the saint's body to his parents, who buried him near the place of execution. The crowd came to pray at his tomb, and the air was full of groans and lamentation. Three days later, the Governor sent soldiers to remove the body and bury it elsewhere, fearing a popular insurrection. The following day, the crowd found the tomb opened and emptied. At once the rumour spread that the Supreme Judge had sent angels to carry away the saint's mortal remains, in which lived on Earth a portion of the Divine Spirit. When this rumour reached the ears of Pilate, he became angry and forbade anyone, under the pain of slavery and death, to pronounce the name of Issa, or to pray to the Lord for him. In spite of this command, the people continued to weep and to glorify aloud their master. Many were captured, tortured and executed.

Issa's disciples fled from Israel and dispersed themselves among the heathen. They preached that they should renounce their sins, consider the salvation of their souls, and of the perfect felicity awaiting humanity in that immaterial world of light, where in repose and in all His purity, the Great Creator dwells in majesty. The pagans, their kings and warriors, listened to these preachers and abandoned their absurd beliefs. They left their priests and idols to celebrate the praise of the all-wise Creator of the Universe, the King of kings, whose heart is filled with infinite mercy.

Amen.

So ends the Gospel of Issa discovered by Nicolai Notovitch at the Hemis Monastery in Tibet. As with the Aquarian Gospel, we shall discuss the case for and against the veracity and authenticity of this gospel in a later chapter. However, we also need to read the other scripture in support of the evidence that Jesus visited India and Tibet in the 'missing years'. I refer to the ancient Hindu Bhavishyat Maha Purana, which will also be rendered in a later chapter, but first we must read Notovitch's own resume of his momentous discovery.

Chapter 4

Notovitch's Conclusions

A t the end of his transcription of the Gospel of Issa, Notovitch writes a chapter giving his reasoned conclusions, and a summary of the gospel he has discovered. Here is an edited, cohesive version of this text to assist us in judging Notovitch's veracity and his mental outlook. I have omitted certain opening paragraphs on the very early history of the Hebrew and Chinese religions which are not relevant to our principal quest. His comments on the reasons for the 'missing years' are worthy of note. His understanding of Hinduism and Buddhism, however, is very much rooted in the knowledge of the 19th century. He does not appear to be familiar with Islam and the Ahmadiyya sect's belief that Jesus was never crucified and lived out his life in India after the Resurrection. The whole chapter gives us an insight into his views, personal opinions and speculations on Christianity, as well on the Gospel of Issa.

INTRODUCTION

In reading the life of Issa, Jesus Christ, we are at first struck by the similarity between some of its principal passages and the biblical narrative; while on the other hand, we also find equally remarkable contradictions, which constitute the difference between the Buddhist version and that found in the New Testament.

To explain this singularity, we must take into account the period in which the facts were recorded. The doctrine of Buddha Gautama, who lived in the 6th century BC, was written on parchment in the Pali language. At this epoch there already existed in India many thousands of Buddhist manuscripts, the compiling of which must have taken a considerable number of years. Hindu chroniclers, thanks to their alphabet, were also able to preserve a concise narrative of events accomplished in their midst, as well as reports received from the many merchants who had visited foreign lands. It is necessary to note here, that during this period of antiquity, as in our own days, oriental public life was concentrated in the bazaars, where the events of the day, and the news from foreign nations, were propagated by caravans of merchants, who readily told all that they had seen and heard on their journey in exchange for sustenance. In fact this was their main means of livelihood.

The commerce of India with Egypt, and later with the Mediterranean, also included Jerusalem, where even as early as the days of King Solomon, Hindu caravans brought precious metals and all that was necessary for the construction of the Temple. Merchandise also came to Jerusalem by sea from other countries, and was unloaded in the port of

Jaffa which still stands. The chronicles I discovered were written before, during, and after Christ; although no attention was paid to Jesus during his sojourn in India, where he came as a simple pilgrim to study the Brahman and Buddhist laws. Later, however, the events which had aroused Israel were related in India; these chroniclers, after having committed to writing all they had just heard concerning the prophet Issa, whom an oppressed nation had followed, and who had been executed by the order of Pilate, remembered that this same Issa had recently lived among them and studied in their midst, and that he had then returned to his own country. A deep interest was immediately aroused concerning this man who had so rapidly gained in importance in their eyes, and they at once began an investigation into his birth, his past, and every detail of his existence.

The two manuscripts read to me by the lama of the Hemis Monastery, were compiled from diverse copies written in the Tibetan tongue, translated from rolls belonging to the Lhasa library and brought from India, Nepal and Maghada 200 years after Christ. These were placed in a convent standing on Mount Marbour, near Lhasa, where the Dalai Lama now resides.

These rolls were written in the Pali tongue, which certain lamas study carefully so that they may translate the sacred writings from that language into the Tibetan dialect. The chroniclers were Buddhists belonging to the sect of Buddha Gautama.

The information contained about Jesus Christ is oddly mixed, without relation or coherence with other events of that period. Without preliminary details or explanation, the manuscript begins by announcing that, in the very year of the death of Christ, a few merchants just returned from Judea have brought back the information that a just man named Issa, an Israelite, after having been twice acquitted by his judges – as was the man of God – was finally put to death at the instigation of the pagan governor, Pilate, who feared that Jesus would take advantage of his popularity to re-establish the Kingdom of Israel and expel its conquerors from the land.

Then comes the somewhat incoherent tale of Jesus preaching among the Guebers and other pagans, evidently written in the year following the death of Christ, in whom there is a growing interest. In one of these stories, the merchants relate what is known about the origin of Jesus and of his family, while another gives the story of the expulsion of his partisans and the bitter persecutions they endured.

It is not until the end of the second volume is reached, that we find the first categorical affirmation of the chronicler where he declares that Issa is blessed by God and the best of all men; that he is the chosen one of the great Brahma, the man in whom is incarnated the spirit detached from the Supreme Being at a period determined by fate.

Having explained that Issa was the son of poor parents and of Israelite extraction, the chronicler makes a slight digression with the object of telling us who were the children of Israel.

These fragments of the life of Issa, I have disposed of in chronological order, endeavouring to give them a character of unity totally wanting in the original form.

I leave it to the scholars, philosophers and theologians, the task of searching the cause of contradictions that may be found between the 'Unknown Life of Issa', which I make public, and the story told by the Evangelists. But I am inclined to believe that nobody will hesitate to acknowledge that this version, recorded within three or four years after the death of Christ from the testimony of eyewitnesses, is more likely to bear the stamp of truth than the narratives of the Evangelists, who wrote at diverse epochs, and so long a time after these events took place, and that we cannot be astonished if the facts have been altered or distorted.

The misfortunes that poured upon the Israelites from the Egyptians, and the afflictions that thereafter embittered their days were, according to the chronicler, more than sufficient reasons for God to look with pity upon his people; and wishing to come their aid, He resolved to descend upon Earth under the guise of a prophet, that He might lead them back into the path of salvation.

The condition of things at that period therefore justified the belief that the coming of Jesus was signalled, immanent and necessary. This explains why the Buddhist traditions declare that the Eternal Spirit detached itself from the Eternal Being and was incarnated in the new-born child of a pious and noble family.

The Buddhists, no doubt, as well as the Evangelists, wished to indicate thereby that the child belonged to the Royal House of David; but the text of the gospel, according to which the 'child was conceived by the Holy Ghost', may be interpreted in two ways, while according to the doctrine of Buddha, which is more in conformity with the laws of nature, the Spirit incarnated itself in a child that was already born, whom God blessed and chose to accomplish his mission here on Earth.

THE MISSING YEARS

At this point there is a great void in the traditions of the Evangelists who, whether through ignorance or negligence, tell us nothing of his infancy, his youth, and his education! They begin the history of Jesus with his first sermon, that is when at the age of 30, he returned to his own country. All that is said by the Evangelists in regard to the infancy of Jesus is totally void of precision: 'And the child grew, and waxed strong in spirit, filled with wisdom; and the grace of God was upon him', says one of the sacred authors St Luke, and again: 'And the child grew, and waxed strong in spirit, and was in the deserts till the day of his shewing unto Israel.'

As the Evangelists compiled their works long after the death of Jesus, it is presumed that they merely consigned to writing the narratives that had come to them of the principal events of the life of Jesus.

The Buddhists, however, who compiled their chronicles immediately after the Passion, and who had the advantage of gathering the most accurate information on all points that interested them, give us a complete and exhaustive description of the life of Jesus.

In those unhappy days, when the struggle for existence seems to have destroyed all notion of God, the people of Israel were bowed down under the double oppression of the ambitious Herod, and of the avaricious despotic Romans. Then as now, the Hebrews placed all their hope in providence, which, they believed, would send them the inspired man who was to deliver them from their physical and moral sufferings. Time passed on, however, and no one took the initiative in a revolt against the tyranny of the governing power.

During this period of anxiety and hope, the people of Israel completely forgot that there existed in their midst a poor Israelite [Joseph or Yeshua], who was a direct descendant of their King David. This man married a young girl [Mary], who gave birth to a miraculous child [Joseph or Yeshua]. Faithful to their traditions of devotion and respect for the race of their kings, the Hebrews on hearing of this birth, flocked to see the child and congratulate the happy father. It is evident that Herod did not remain in ignorance for long of what had taken place; and he feared that when the child had grown to manhood, he might take advantage of his popularity to regain the throne of his ancestors. He, therefore, sought the child, whom the Israelites endeavoured to shield from the anger of the king. Herod then ordered the abominable massacre of children, hoping that Jesus might perish in this vast human hecatomb. But the family of Joseph, having obtained information of the terrible execution contemplated by Herod, fled into Egypt.

Some time later the family returned to their native land. The child had grown during these journeys in which his life had been more than once exposed. Then as now, the Oriental Israelites commenced to instruct their children at the age of five or six years old. Forced to remain in concealment, the parents never allowed their son to leave their roof, and the latter no doubt spent his time in studying the sacred writings, so that on his return to Judea, he was far in advance of the boys of his own age, which greatly astonished the learned men. He was then in his 13th year, the age at which, according to the Jewish law, a young man attains his majority and has the right to marry, as well as to fulfil his religious duties on an equal footing with adults.

His royal origin, his rare intelligence and the extensive studies to which he had applied himself, caused him to be looked upon as an excellent suitor, and the most noble and rich sought him as a son-in-law. But the studious youth, seemingly detached from all things corporal and devoured by a thirst for knowledge, stealthily left his father's house and fled to India with a departing caravan.

FLIGHT TO INDIA

It is to be supposed that Jesus Christ chose India, first, because Egypt made part of the Roman possessions at that period, and then because an active trade with India had spread marvellous reports in regard to the majestic character and inconceivable riches of art and science in that wonderful country where the aspirations of civilized nations still tend in our own age.

Here the Evangelists again lose the thread of the terrestrial life of Jesus. St Luke says, 'He was in the desert till the day of his shewing unto Israel', which conclusively proves that no one knew where the young man had gone, to so suddenly reappear 16 years later. Once in India, the country of marvels, Jesus began by frequenting the temples of the Jains. There still exists in the peninsula of Hindustan a sect which bears the name of Jainism. It forms a link, as it were, between Buddhism and Brahmanism, and preaches the destruction of all other beliefs, which they declare to be steeped in error. It dates back to the 7th century before Christ, and its name is derived from the word Jaine (conquering), which it assumes as a symbol of triumph over its rivals.

Amazed at the young man's brilliant intellect, the Jains begged him to remain in their midst; but Jesus left them to settle at Juggernaut, one of the principal cities of the Brahmins, and enjoying great religious importance at the time of Christ, where he devoted himself to the study of treatises on religion and philosophy, etc. A cherished tradition claims that the ashes of the illustrious Brahman, Krishna are preserved here in the hollow of a tree near a magnificent temple visited by thousands every year. A library, rich in Sanskrit books and precious religious manuscripts, is also found at Juggernaut.

Jesus spent six years at this place, studying the language of the country and Sanskrit, which enabled him to dive deeply into all religious doctrines, philosophy, medicine and mathematics. He found much to condemn in Brahmin laws and customs, and entered into public debates with the Brahmins, who strove to convince him of the sacred character of their established customs. Among other things, Jesus particularly censured the injustice of humiliating the labourer, and of not only depriving him of the benefits to come, but also of contesting his right to hear religious readings. Jesus began to preach to the Sudras, the lowest caste of slaves, saying that God is One, according to their own laws, that all that is, exists through Him, that all are equal in His sight, and that the Brahmins had obscured the great principle of monotheism in perverting the words of Brahman Himself, and insisting to excess on the exterior ceremonies of the religion.

These are the terms, according to the Brahmin doctrine, in which God speaks of Himself to the angels: 'I have been since all eternity and shall be eternally. I am the first cause of all that exists in the East and in the West, in the North and in the South, above and below, in heaven and hell. I am older than all things. I am the Spirit and the creation of the universe and its creator. I am Almighty, I am the God of gods, the King of kings; I am Parabrahman, the great soul of the universe.'

After the world had appeared by the mere wish of Parabrahman, God created man, whom he divided into four classes, according to their destiny, Brahmins (priests), Kshatriyas (warriors), Vaisyas (merchants and farmers) and Sudras (labourers). The Brahmins alone occupy the position of priests and preachers, and sole commentators on the Vedas, and should adopt celibacy. The warriors are entrusted with the sacred mission of defending and protecting society. The kings and commanders of armies belong to this class of knights, and enjoy cordial relations with the Brahmins. The merchants and farmers are responsible for the commercial life of the country, with limited rights to the reading of the Vedas only on feast days. The Sudras are the humble servants and slaves of the other three castes. They are forbidden to attend the reading of the Vedas; and to come into contact with them means contamination, hence the name 'untouchables'. They are wretched beings, robbed of most human rights.

It is therefore easy to understand the veneration of Jesus by the Vaisyas and the Sudras, who notwithstanding the threats of the Brahmins, never abandoned him. In his sermons, Jesus not only inveighed against the injustice of depriving a man of his right to be considered as such, while an idol was worshiped, but he also denounced the many different gods of the Brahmins. He denied the existence of all these gods which obscured the monotheistic principle of One God. Seeing that the people were beginning to embrace the doctrines of Jesus, whom they had hoped to gain on their side, and who was now their adversary, the Brahmins resolved to assassinate him; but being warned in time by his devoted servants, he fled and took refuge in the mountains of Nepal.

Buddhism had already taken deep root in this country at that period. This teaching was remarkable for its moral principles and ideas on the nature of divinity, which brought man and nature, and men among themselves, nearer together. The founder, Sakyamuni, was born 1,500 years before Christ at Kapila, the capital of his father's kingdom, near Nepal in the Himalayas. He evinced a strong attachment to religion from childhood and, notwithstanding his father's objections and disapproval, left the palace in which he lived with all its luxuries. He immediately began to preach against the Brahmins, meanwhile purifying their doctrine. When he died his ashes were distributed among the cities in which his new doctrine had replaced Brahminism.

Jesus spent six years among the Buddhists, where he found the principles of monotheism still in their purity. Having reached the age of 26 he thought about his native country, which laboured under a foreign yoke. He therefore resolved to return there. While journeying, he continued to preach against idolatry, human sacrifice and religious errors, exhorting the people to acknowledge and adore God, the father of all creatures, whom He cherishes equally, the masters as well as the slaves, for they are all His children, to whom He had given His beautiful universe as a common inheritance. The sermons of Jesus often produced a deep impression upon the nations he visited, where he braved many dangers instigated by the priests, but was as often protected by the idolaters who, only the day before, had sacrificed their children to the idols.

THE RETURN TO ISRAEL

While crossing Persia, Jesus almost caused an uprising among the followers of Zoroaster. Fearing the vengeance of the people, however, the priests dared not assassinate him, but had recourse to a ruse instead, and drove him from the town during the night, hoping he might be devoured by wild beasts. But Jesus escaped this peril and arrived safe and sound in the land of Israel.

Saint Luke says, 'Jesus was about 30 years of age when he began to exercise his ministry'. According to the Buddhist chronicler, Jesus would have commenced to preach in his

29th year. All his sermons that the Evangelists do not mention and which have been preserved by the Buddhists, are remarkable for their character of divine grandeur. The fame of the new preacher spread rapidly through the country, and Jerusalem impatiently awaited his coming. When he drew near to the Holy City, all the inhabitants went forth to meet him and conducted him in triumph to the Temple, which is in conformity with Christian tradition. The chiefs and the learned men who listened, admired his sermons and rejoiced at the beneficent impression produced on the multitude by his sublime words.

But Pontius Pilate, Governor of the country, did not see the matter in the same light. Zealous agents reported to him that Jesus announced the near approach of a new kingdom, the reestablishment of the throne of Israel, and that he called himself the Son of God, sent to revive the courage of Israel, for he, King of Judea, would soon ascend the throne of his ancestors.

Alarmed at these rumours, Pilate assembled the learned men and the elders of the people, charging them to interdict Jesus from public preaching and condemn him in the Temple under the accusation of apostasy. This was the easiest way of ridding himself of a dangerous man whose royal origin was known to Pilate, and whose fame was growing among the people.

At Pilate's command, the Sanhedrin assembled and cited Jesus to appear before its tribunal. At the conclusion of the inquest, the members of the Sanhedrin announced to Pilate that his suspicions were groundless. The Buddhist chronicle only tends to confirm this sympathy which indubitably existed between Jesus, the young preacher, and the elders of the people of Israel; hence their response: 'We do not judge a just man.'

Pilate was not reassured, however, and sought another opportunity to summon Jesus before a regular tribunal; to this end he sent many spies to watch him, and he was at length apprehended. According to the Evangelists, it was the Pharisees and Hebrews who sought to have Jesus put to death, while the Buddhist chronicler positively declares that Pilate alone must be held responsible. This version is much more likely than the account given by the Evangelists; the Roman conquerors of Judea being unable to tolerate, any longer, a man who announced to the people their near deliverance from the foreign yoke!

Seeing that torture did not bring about the desired confession, Pilate commanded his servants to proceed to the utmost cruelty; that his death might be brought about by exhaustion. Jesus, however, suffered with an unflinching endurance all the refinements of cruelty received at the hands of his torturers. Jesus having undergone the secret inquisition, the elders were much displeased, and resolved to intercede in his favour and ask that he be freed before the Passover festival.

Foiled in the object of their demand by Pilate, they determined to insist upon having him brought before the tribunal, so certain were they of his acquittal, which seemed fully assured since the entire people ardently desired it. In the eyes of the priests, Jesus was a saint belonging to the House of David, and his unjust detention, or what was still more grave, his condemnation, would cast a deep gloom upon the solemnity of the great national festival of Passover. On hearing the refusal of their demand, they begged that the trial should take place before the feast. This time Pilate acceded to their wishes, but also ordered that two thieves should be tried at the same time. By this means Pilate strove to belittle, in the eyes of the people, the importance that might be attached to a judgement rendered against an innocent man if he were tried alone, thus leaving the nation under the sad impression of a verdict dictated beforehand; while on the contrary, the simultaneous judgement of Jesus and the two thieves would almost efface the injustice committed against one of the accused.

The accusation was based upon the depositions of hired witnesses.

During the trial, Pilate used the words of Jesus, who preached the Kingdom of Heaven, to justify the accusation against him. He relied upon the effect produced by the replies of Jesus, as well as on his own personal authority to influence the members of the tribunal to not examine too minutely the details of the case before them, to obtain the desired verdict.

After hearing the perfectly natural reply of the judges, that the words of Jesus only proved a sentiment diametrically opposed to the accusation, and that he could not be condemned, Pilate had recourse to the only means left to him. That was, to the deposition of an informer, who, in the governor's judgement, could not fail to produce a deep impression on the judges. The wretch, who was none other than Judas, then formally accused Jesus of having incited the people to rebellion.

There followed a scene of the grandest sublimity. While Judas gave utterance to his testimony, Jesus turned to him, and having blessed him, said, 'Thou shall be forgiven, for what thou sayest cometh not of thee'. Then turning to the governor, he continued: 'Why lower thy dignity and teach thy inferiors to live in falsehood, since, even without this, thou hast the power to condemn an innocent man?'

With these touching and sublime words, Jesus Christ manifests himself in all his grandeur, first in showing the informer that he has betrayed his conscience, then forgiving him. Turning next to Pilate he censured him for having recourse to proceedings so degrading to his dignity to obtain his condemnation.

The accusation brought by Jesus against Pilate caused the latter to completely forget his position and the prudence he should display. He therefore imperiously demanded the condemnation of Jesus at the hands of the judges and, as if to assert the unlimited power he enjoyed, the acquittal of the two thieves.

Finding this demand to discharge the two thieves and condemn Jesus, though innocent, too unjust to comply with, the judges refused to commit this double crime against their conscience and their laws; but being too weak to struggle against a man who had the power to give a final verdict, and seeing him determined to rid himself of a person who rivalled the Roman authorities, they left him to pronounce the judgement he so ardently desired. That they might not be censured by the people, who could not have forgiven so unjust a judgement, they washed their hands as they came out of the tribunal chamber, showing thereby that they were innocent of the death of Jesus whom the multitude adored.

About ten years ago I read an article on Judas in a German journal, *Fremdenblatt*, in which the author endeavoured to show that the informer had been Jesus' best friend. It would seem that it was through love for his master that Judas betrayed him, in his blind belief in the words of the Saviour, who said that his kingdom would come after his crucifixion. But when he beheld him on the Cross, after vainly awaiting his immediate resurrection, Judas found himself incapable of bearing his remorse and hanged himself.

It is useless to elaborate on this lucubration, which is certainly original.

To return to the scriptural narrative and the Buddhist chronicle, it seems quite probable that the hired informer may have been Judas, although the Buddhist version is silent on this point. As to the theory that remorse of conscience drove the informer to the taking of his own life, I place little credence on it.

It is to be presumed that the governor took this matter into his own hands, as is sometimes done in our days, when it is imperative to keep from the people a grave and compromising secret which such a man might easily betray without heeding the consequences. Judas was probably hanged in order to prevent him from ever revealing that the testimony on which Jesus was condemned emanated from the governor himself.

THE CRUCIFIXION

On the day of the Crucifixion, a large body of Roman soldiers was stationed about the Cross to prevent the people from rescuing the object of their worship. In this circumstance, Pilate displayed extraordinary firmness and resolution. But although, owing to his precautions, an uprising was averted, he could not prevent the people from weeping over the downfall of their hopes, which died with the last descendant of the House of David. The entire population went to adore the tomb of Jesus, and although we have no precise details of the first days after the Passion, we may easily imagine the scenes that must have taken place. It is only reasonable to suppose that the prudent lieutenant of the Roman Caesar, seeing that the tomb of Jesus was becoming a shrine of universal lamentations and the object of national mourning, and fearing that the memory of this just man might excite discontent and perhaps arouse the entire population against their foreign yoke, should have taken all possible means to divert the public mind from the recollection of Jesus. For three days the soldiers placed on guard at the tomb were the butt of the jeers and maledictions of the people who, braving the danger, came in throngs to adore the great martyr. Pilate therefore ordered his soldiers to remove the body during the night, when the pilgrimages had ceased, and inter it clandestinely in another place, leaving the first tomb open and unguarded, that the people might see that Jesus had disappeared.

However, Pilate failed to accomplish this end; for, on the following day, not finding the body of their master in the sepulchre, the Hebrews, who were very superstitious and believed in miracles, declared him resurrected. How this legend came to be generally accepted, we do not know. However this may be, since the day this legend became known to all, no one has had the strength of mind to point out its impossibility.

As concerns the Resurrection itself, it must be remarked that according to the Buddhists, the soul of the just man was united to the Eternal Being, while the Evangelists and Apostles were wise in giving a clear description of the Resurrection; for otherwise, had the miracle been less material, their sermons would not have been stamped, in the eyes of the people, with divine authority: that character so manifestly divine, which Christianity retains to this day, as being the only religion capable of maintaining the people in a state of sublime enthusiasm, of softening their savage instincts, and of bringing them nearer to the great and simple nature which God has confided, it is said, to the feeble dwarf called man.

So, Notovitch's summary, his discovery and somewhat controversial conclusion ends somewhat abruptly. He obviously had no knowledge regarding Islam's standpoint on the Crucifixion and the later escape to India and Kashmir. Before we evaluate Notovitch's testimony and discovery fully, we must look at other theories as to what really happened in those mysterious 'missing years'. This we will attempt in the following chapters. Meanwhile, we must examine the Hindu scriptural evidence for Jesus' appearance in India.

Chapter 5

The Bhavishyat Maha Purana and the Natha Namavali Sutra

These are two different scriptural texts. First we have the Bhavishyat Maha Purana and then the Natha Namavali Sutra.

I shall first paraphrase the ancient and revered Hindu scripture, the Bhavishyat Maha Purana, into a readable form based on the several translations that exist. The many Puranas are sacred to the Hindus. They relate the legendary history and mythology of the different gods and goddesses that make up the Hindu pantheon. They rank only second to the Vedas in their importance, and are much revered by the various adherents of the different faiths, which collectively constitute the Hindu religion. From the 4th century BC until the 17th century AD they have been constantly extended by the addition of further narratives. The current collection is 18 volumes, and all in Sanskrit. The ninth volume, the Bhavishyat Maha Purana, has been attributed to the sage, Suta, probably around AD 115, and contains the report that describes Jesus' visit to India. The Maharajah of

Kashmir sent the manuscript to the Research Institute in Poona for verification, and it was published in Bombay in 1910. The Purana states that Israelites came to live in India and then in verses 17–32 describes Jesus' appearance in India.

THE BHAVISHYAT MAHA PURANA

Ruling over the Aryans was a king called Salivahana (between AD 49 and 50), the grandson of Vikramaditya, who occupied the throne of his father. He defeated the invading Chinese, Parthians, Scythians and Bactrians. He punished them severely and took away their wealth. Salivahana then established the boundaries dividing the separate countries of the Mlecchas (Barbarians or Non-Hindus) and the Aryans. In this way Sindusthan came to be known as the greatest country. He established the Kingdom of the Mlecchas beyond the Sindhu river and to the west.

Once upon a time this subduer of the Scythians went towards Himatunga and in the middle of the Huna country (Hunadesh – the area near Manasa Sarovara or Mount Kailash in western Tibet), the powerful king saw a handsome man who was living on a snow-white mountain. The man's complexion was golden and his clothes were white. The king asked, 'Who are you?' The man answered, 'You should know that I am Ishaputra, Son of God and I am born of a virgin. I am the teacher of true religion to the barbarian Mlecchas which are the Absolute Truth.'

Hearing this, the king enquired, 'What are the chief religious teachings in your opinion?'

Hearing these questions of Salivahana, Ishaputra replied,

'Oh King, when the destruction of the truth, at the end of the Golden Age, occurred in the depraved land of the heathen, I appeared as Masiha, the Messiah, after initiation by the goddess Ishamasi, the Lord Messiah, and came to this country of degraded people where there are no rules and regulations. Finding that fearful irreligious condition of the barbarians spreading from Mleccha-Desha, I have taken to prophecy. Please hear, Oh King, the religious principles I have established among the barbarians. The living soul is subject to good and evil contamination. The mind should be purified by adopting proper conduct and performance of japa, chanting the holy names, to attain the highest purity. Just as the immovable Sun attracts, from all directions, the elements of all living beings, the Lord of the Solar Region, Almighty God, who is immutable and all perfect, attracts the hearts of all living creatures. So by following regulations, speaking truthful words, by mental harmony and by meditation, Oh descendant of Manu, they should worship that immovable Lord. Having placed the eternally pure and auspicious form of the Supreme Lord in my heart, O protector of the earth planet, I preach these principles through the Mlecchas' own faith and thus my name became "Isha-Masiha" (Jesus the Messiah).'

After hearing these words and paying obeisance to that sage who is worshipped by the wicked, the king humbly requested him to stay there in the dreadful land of Mlecchas.

So ends the second chapter entitled, 'the age of Salivahara' of the story of Kali Yuga of the Caturyuga Khanda also called Pratisarga-parva of the wonderful Bhavishya Maha Purana.

Professor Dr Fida Hassnain Levi has written several important books on Jesus in India, published in Kashmir. In these it is stated that the Natha Sect own an ancient Hindu Sutra, known as the Natha-Namavali, still preserved by them. In this text they refer to Jesus as Isha Natha. Here is a rendition.

THE NATHA NAMAVALI SUTRA

Isha Natha came to India at the age of 14. Afterwards he returned to his own homeland and began to preach. Soon, however, his brutal and materialistic countrymen conspired against him, and he was crucified, but before the crucifixion Isha Natha entered samadhi [a deep trance]. Observing him in this way, the Jews assumed he was dead and buried him in a tomb. Simultaneously one of Isha Natha's Himalayan teachers, the great Chetan Natha, was in samadhi, and he saw in a vision the tortures undergone by Isha Natha. He therefore, with his sidhis [yogic powers], made his body as light as air, and transported himself to Jerusalem. On arrival there was thunder and lightning for God was angry with the Jews, and the world trembled. Then Chetan Natha took the body of Isha Natha and aroused him from his deep trance, and later led him back to India. Isha Natha later built an ashram in the foothills of the Himalayas.

To this day these Natha yogis still sing *bhajans* (devotional hymns) referring to John the Baptist.

As with the Aquarian Gospel and the Gospel of Issa, the ancient Purana (where the name Ishaputra bears some resemblance to the Tibetan Issa, and the Aramaic Yeshua), along with the Natha Namavali Sutra, will be fully discussed in my final chapter as possible evidence for Jesus having visited India and Tibet.

Chapter 6

The Parallels Between Christianity, Hinduism and Buddhism

There are many striking similarities between Buddhism and Christianity. Scholars and theologians have often come to the conclusion that Jesus could well have, or even must have, been in contact with Buddhists, by visiting Tibet and India in his 'missing years' or meeting with them in Jerusalem. Buddhism predates Christianity by around 500 years, so if Jesus was to investigate other great existing world faiths, apart from his native Judaism, Buddhism would have been an obvious choice. Hinduism, the oldest of the world religions, originated from the Vedic civilization, from which the Vedas and Upanishads sprang. These are believed to predate Jesus' life on earth by at least 3,000 years, and would also have been of tremendous interest to him.

Let us look at some of these similarities in more detail.

Buddhism

The aim of Buddhism is to become 'an awakened one', and a similar metaphor is often used by Christ when he refers to man being asleep. 'Awake you who sleep, and Christ shall give you light', (Ephesians 5:14) is the clarion call of early Christianity. The Dhammapada also uses this metaphor to describe man's spiritual condition. 'Earnest among the thoughtless, awake among the sleepers!' (II:29)

Both religions see man's 'suffering' to be at the root of his spiritual dilemma on Earth. Universal love and compassion, under all circumstances, for the wretched human situation, are stressed equally strongly by both teachers. A study of Jesus' Beatitudes and his gospel teachings shows remarkable correspondences with both the Four Noble Truths and The Eightfold Path, with their emphasis on the causes of suffering and the remedies. They both preach limitless compassion and all-embracing, unconditional love, especially for the poor and downtrodden. They both stress the need for moral and ethical purification to realize nirvana or the Kingdom of Heaven within. They both preach in parables and are highly critical of the priestly castes. For example, similar parables such as the 'widow's mite' have been used by both teachings.

There is considerable literature, accumulated over the centuries, pointing out the close affinities between Buddhist and Christian attitudes in their teachings. Both seek to effect the deliverance of mankind from sin, and cut off the sources of retributive suffering and continued sinfulness. Both present a divine personage as an object of faith, whom in his human life devoted himself to teaching. Between the traditions of their founders' personal experiences, the growth of their disciples' fellowship, their ethical teaching and their missionary aims, the two religions show marked resemblances. Both the Buddha and Jesus link their teachings with the Infinite and Eternal Source of all existence. Both present ultimate salvation through participation in the Divine Nature, and picture its realization in the adoring communion of the soul with the founder of their faith. Both masters sought to express the value of eternal life, conceived in the sublime terms of truth, purity and love. They share a sublime love for a fallen humanity, and preach the urgent message for men and women to wake up from spiritual sleep, if not spiritual death!

The idealist philosopher Arthur Schopenhauer, who studied the Upanishads and scriptures of early Buddhism and is considered to be the bridge between Eastern and Western philosophy, made no secret of his view that the New Testament was strongly influenced by Indian and Buddhist thought. And that the asceticism, the ethical values, the pessimistic undertone and the idea that the divine consciousness incarnates in an earthly form, entail amazing correspondences with either an Indian or more likely a Buddhist source. He wrote in his *Parerga and Paralipomena* that 'although on the surface, i.e. in the realm of emotion, they may be diametrically contradictory: one ignoring a personal God, and the other proclaiming him; one teaching self-salvation, assisted by a saviour; the other preaching salvation through Christ alone, seconded by one's prayers and efforts; one asserting a past eternity of transmigration that must end in Nirvana; the other ignoring the past, but clinging to a future eternity of a personal redeemed life. Yet, deep in the region of truth, the two are one: both proclaim the necessity of a second death, a death of the petty egotistic self: "whoso seeketh his soul shall lose it, but he that loseth it shall find it." (John 17:22, 23) Both maintain, in different ways – one emotionally, and the other intellectually – that this false egotistic self is unreal, that we metaphysical islands, were once part of a continent and may yet be so again.'

The doctrine of Buddhist and Hindu reincarnation was taught by the influential 3rd-century Christian theologian Origen, but the sixth Council of Constantinople decided to condemn Origen for this teaching. Some modern writers such as Thich Nhat Hanh, the celebrated Vietnamese Buddhist, writing in his book *Living Buddha, Living Christ*, argues that the doctrine of resurrection does have to do with reincarnation. According to him, an immortal soul does not need to be resurrected. It is the body that does. Therefore according to the Christian teaching of the Last Judgement everyone will have his or her body resurrected. So elements of reincarnation are certainly present in Christianity.

Rudolph Seydell, Professor of Philosophy at Leipzig University, who wrote a masterly evaluation of Schopenhauer's contribution to philosophy, also wrote two scholarly studies illustrating that the gospels are full of significant parallels with Buddhist texts. Paul Ambroise Bigandet, the Catholic Bishop of Ramatha, writes on this question, 'that there are many moral precepts equally commanded and enforced in common by both creeds. It will not be rash to assert that most of the moral truths prescribed in the gospel are to be met with in the Buddhistic scriptures.' And Bishop Jean Paul Hilaire writes in a similar vein when he states that, 'He [Buddha] requires humility, disregard of worldly wealth, patience and resignation in adversity, love to enemies ... non-resistance to evil, confession of sins and conversion as does Christ.'

A significant book on this whole topic, entitled *Jesus and Buddha: Parallel Sayings*, has been written by the distinguished biblical scholar Marcus Borg. Borg has found hundreds of parallel quotations between the sayings of Jesus Christ in the New Testament and the Buddha in the Buddhist scriptures. In his introduction he outlines the similarities that exist not only in their ethical teachings, but in the purpose of their mission, and to some extent their personal history. To demonstrate the parallels his chapters consist of many quotations. On compassion; both teachers advocated the Golden Rule, of treating others as you want them to treat you, and emphasized the virtues and powers inherent in love. On wisdom, where the inner life is far more important than the outer image. A critique of materialism, where the acquisition of wealth is a handicap on the way to salvation, and stressing the virtues of poverty and the ascetic life. On temptation, where both teachers demonstrate their personal resistance to this spiritual challenge. On salvation, stressing the essential need for moral purity to realize nirvana or the Kingdom of Heaven within. On the future, where they prophesy that their teachings would continue after their death, leading mankind to 'the renewal of all things'. On miracles, where they both exhibit extraordinary powers over nature. On discipleship, demanding great faith and persistence in one's personal pilgrimage. On personal attributes, where both demonstrate divine tendencies, well above the level of ordinary human beings. And on their life stories where both have miraculous births and are spiritual prodigies.

There is, however, an earlier book than Marcus Borg's modern study. Albert J Edmunds made the study of parallels between the two religions his life work. The first edition of his seminal, monumental *Buddhist and Christian Gospels: Being Gospel Parallels from Pali Texts*, appeared in 1902 and caused considerable excitement and interest in both the Christian and Buddhist worlds. It was followed by a second edition in 1904 and a new edition was written with the assistance of the Buddhist scholar M Anesaki in 1905. In his introduction he details the considerable maritime and overland trade between ancient Greece, the Roman Empire and the Far East, particularly India. Edmunds found considerable parallels between the gospels and ancient Pali texts which predate Christianity by several hundred years. As they are of great relevance to the thesis that Jesus may well have visited India and Tibet, I will quote some of his parallels which indicate how Jesus may well have been influenced by Buddhism, much more than is generally acknowledged by members of both religions today.

In Luke 6:31 we read: 'As ye would that men should do unto you, do ye also to them likewise.' In the Dhammapada, a book of Buddhist hymns, translated by Max Muller in his monumental series *Sacred Books of the East* Volume X Part 1 (page 36) we read: 'All men tremble at the rod, all men fear death: Putting oneself in the place of others, kill not nor cause to kill. All men tremble at the rod, unto all men life is dear: Doing as one would be done by, kill not nor cause to kill.'

In Luke 4:27–28 we read: 'But I say unto you which hear, Love your enemies, do good to them that hate you, bless them that curse you, pray for them that despitefully use you.' In the Buddhist hymns 3–5 we read: 'He abused me, he beat me, overcame me, robbed me. In those who harbour such thoughts their anger is not calmed. Not by anger are angers in this world ever calmed: By absence of anger are angers calmed. This is an ancient doctrine.' And in Hymn 223 we read: 'Let one conquer wrath by absence of wrath, let one conquer wrong by goodness, let one conquer the mean man by a gift, and a liar by the truth.' There is a remarkable parallel between Matthew 6:19, 20 when the gospel says: 'Lay not up for yourselves treasures upon the Earth, where moth and rust doth consume, and where thieves break through and steal: but lay up for yourselves treasures in heaven, where neither moth nor rust doth consume, and where thieves do not break through nor steal.' And the Treasure Chapter in the Short Recital, where the Buddhist scripture says: 'Let the wise man do righteousness: A treasure that others can share not, which no thief can steal; a treasure which passeth not away.' This 'treasure metaphor' is echoed in Luke 12:21, 33: 'So is he that layeth up treasure for himself, and is not rich toward God ... Sell that ye have, and give alms; make for yourselves purses which wax not old, a treasure in the heavens that faileth not, where no thief draweth near, neither moth destroyeth.'

Here are more of Edmunds' discoveries: 'Beware of false prophets, which come to you in sheep's clothing but inwardly are ravening wolves.' (Matthew 7:15) 'And the Lord said unto him, "Now do ye Pharisees cleanse the outside of the cup and the platter; but your inward part is full of extortion and wickedness."' (Luke 11:39) Buddhist hymn 394: 'What use to thee is matted hair, o fool! What use the goat-skin garment? Within thee there is ravening; the outside thou makest clean.'

Matthew 3:14: 'John would have hindered him, saying, "I have need to be baptized of thee, and comest thou to me?"' John 4:2: 'Jesus himself baptized not, but his disciples.' In the

Buddhist Long Collection, Dialogue 16, from Book of the Great Decease, we read: 'Now Subhaddo the hermit said unto the venerable Anando: "Lucky friend Anando, very fortunate friend Nando are ye who have been here sprinkled with the sprinkling of discipleship in the presence of the Master!"'

Luke 6:20: 'He lifted up his eyes on his disciples, and said: "Blessed are ye poor: for yours is the kingdom of God."' Matthew 8:20: 'The foxes have holes, and the birds of the heaven have nests; but the Son of man hath not where to lay his head.' Buddhist hymn 200: 'Ah! Live we happily in sooth, we who have nothing: feeders on joy shall we be. Even as the angels of splendour.' Hymn 91: 'The thoughtful struggle onward, and delight not in abode: like swans who leave a lake, do they leave house and home.' Hymn 421: 'Whoso before, behind and in the midst Hath naught his own – possessing nothing, clinging unto naught – Him do I call a Brahmin.'

Mark 7:15: 'Hear me all of you, and understand: there is nothing from without the man, that going into him can defile him: but the things which proceed out of the man are those that defile the man.' Collection of Discourses II:2w: 'Destroying life, killing, cutting, binding, stealing, speaking lies, fraud and deceptions, worthless reading, intercourse with another's wife, – this is defilement.'

Matthew 17:20, 21: 'And he saith unto them, "Because of your little faith: for verily I say unto you, if ye have faith as a grain of mustard seed, ye shall say unto this mountain, remove hence to yonder place; and it shall remove; and nothing shall be impossible unto you."' Buddhist Numerical Collection VI:24: 'a monk endowed with the six qualities can cleave the Himalaya, the monarch of mountains.'

Matthew 17:27: 'Go thou to the sea, and cast a hook, and take up the fish that first cometh up; and when thou hast opened his mouth, thou shalt find a shekel: that take, and give unto them for me and thee.' Buddhist Birth-Story 288, Stanza 1: 'Fishes are worth as much as a thousand pieces. There is no one who could believe this. But to me let them be here seven pence: I would fain buy even this whole string of fishes.'

Mark 8:11, 12: 'And the Pharisees came forth and began to question with him, seeking of him a sign from heaven, tempting him. And he sighed deeply in his spirit and said, "Why does this generation seek a sign? Verily I say unto you, there shall be no sign given unto this generation."' From the Buddhist minor section on discipline V:8: 'Ye are not O monks, to display psychical power or miracle of superhuman kind before the laity. Whoever does so is guilty of a misdemeanour.'

Mark 9:38: 'Jesus said unto him. "If thou canst! All things are possible to him that believeth."' Buddhist Numerical Collection I:17: 'Beings possessed of Right Belief, O monks, upon the dissolution of the body after death, rise again in the world of paradise.'

John 16:33: 'Whatsoever is begotten of God overcometh the world: and this is the victory that hath overcome the world, even our faith. And who is he that overcometh the world, but he that believeth that Jesus is the Son of God?' Buddhist Numerical Collection IV:36: 'I am born in the world, grown up in the world, and having overcome the world, I abide by the same undefiled.'

John 8:12: 'Jesus spake unto them, saying, "I am the light of the world."' John 9:5–7: '"When I am in the world, I am the light of the world." When he had thus spoken, he spat upon the ground, and made clay of his spittle, and anointed his eyes with the clay.' Buddhist Classified Collection LVI:38: 'But when, O monks, a Tathagato, a Holy One, a perfect Buddha ariseth in the world, then is there appearance of great glory and of splendour; gloom and dense darkness are no more: then is there proclamation of the Four Noble Truths; there is preaching thereof, publication, establishment, exposition, analysis, elucidation.' Buddhist Long Collection, Dialogue 16: 'Too soon will the Lord enter Nirvana! Too soon will the Auspicious One enter Nirvana! Too soon will the Light of the World vanish away!'

John 14:6: 'Jesus saith unto him, "I am the way and the truth, and the life: no one cometh unto the father; but by me."' Buddhist Logia Book 923: 'He who sees not the Doctrine sees not me.'

John 11:26: 'Whosoever liveth and believeth in me shall never die.' Buddhist Numerical Collection X:64: 'Monks, those who believe in me are all assured of final salvation.'

John 17:14–16 'I have given them thy word; and the world hated them, because my words are not of the world, even as I am not of the world.' Buddhist Classified Collection XXII:94: 'Monks, even as a blue lotus, a water rose or a white lotus is born in the water, grows up in the water, and stands lifted above it, by the water undefiled: even so, monks, does the Tathagato grow up in the world, and abide in the mastery of the world, by the world undefiled.'

Matthew 24:14: 'This Gospel of the Kingdom shall be preached in the whole world, for a testimony unto all the nations; and then shall the end come.' Buddhist Long Collection, Dialogue 16: 'I shall not pass into Nirvana [i.e. die] till my monks and nuns, my laymen and laywomen, become wise and trained disciples, apt and learned, reciters of the

Doctrine. I shall not pass into Nirvana till this religion of mine is successful, prosperous, widespread, popular, ubiquitous; in a word, made thoroughly public among men.'

Matthew 28:20: 'Lo, I am with you always, even unto the consummation of the age.' Buddhist Long Collection Dialogue 1: 'Monks, the cord of existence is cut off, but the Tathagato's body remains. So long as his body shall remain, then angels and mortals will see him.'

This is only a small sample of the hundreds of parallels found by Marcus Borg and Albert Edmunds. The reader may feel that the many correspondences point to Jesus either having met Buddhists in Tibet and India as Notovitch and Dowling claim, or at least having read their scriptures in Jerusalem during his 'missing years', where they may have been somewhat difficult to find in this outpost of the Roman Empire. Some scholars believe that the Essenes and Theraputae were similarly influenced by Buddhism in their asceticism and doctrines. Of course the styles of the Buddha's and Jesus' rhetoric are very different, as they must be, separated by several centuries and many cultural differences, but the essential truth behind the sayings in many cases is very similar, if not precisely the same.

Of course there are many theological differences between Buddhism, which is essentially a religion termed by theologians as the 'Via Negativa', and Christianity, which is known as the 'Via Positiva'. Putting aside these distinctions, we are left with a striking number of parallel quotations. Of course many argue that the great founders of higher world religions are bound to share a great deal of common experience, which they express in their dissertations and discourses on the Truth. Although this thesis of commonality, the sharing of the highest common factor of spiritual

Truth among mystics – the Perennial Philosophy, as Aldous Huxley termed it – is a probability, it is still inconclusive. Huxley compiled a brilliant anthology entitled *The Perennial Philosophy* to illustrate his point of view. These parallels do, however, suggest a distinct possibility that Jesus knew about Buddhist teachings either by a direct visit to a Buddhist land, such as Tibet, or by meeting practising Buddhists in Jerusalem.

So if, as is surmised, Jesus did actually visit Tibet, he must have studied and immersed himself in Buddhist scriptures. This would have strongly influenced his ministry when he returned to Jerusalem to commence his great mission. In fact, all the great qualities that characterize the Buddhist Bhodhisattva ideal are there to be found in Jesus Christ. *The Wisdom Quarterly: American Buddhist Journal* strongly affirms that Jesus did visit India and Tibet, as in the Gospel of Issa which Notovitch later discovered. They even claim that this knowledge was 'something that was no secret to Vatican elders and Greek Orthodox scholars who inherited redactions of the tradition that very deliberately omitted biblical references to this at the Council of Nicaea.' I cannot, however, find any hard evidence to support this statement in my researches up to now. More significantly, there is the basic attitude of the truly religious man or woman, which must rest on the principle of 'inwardness'. This is stressed by both teachers over and over again. One could fill many books with the correspondences that scholars of comparative religion have discovered. There is no doubt that Jesus, if he did indeed visit Tibet, must have been strongly influenced by the Buddha's teaching, and this would readily explain the striking similarities found between the two great religions, particularly in the ethical and moral dimension.

Hinduism

The background of Christianity and Judaism, like Hinduism and Islam, is Asiatic. These higher religions believe in prophets or messengers of God appearing on Earth in human form. In the teachings of both great religions, Hinduism and Christianity, devotion to God, and His grace and love bestowed in return, are particularly stressed. It is also a known historical fact that the wise men of Persia, the Magi, and the Indian Gymnophysicists, as the Yogis were called by Josephus and the Greeks, visited ancient Athens. Their knowledge also spread to Rome, and then probably on to Jerusalem, part of the Roman Empire. There was always some connection between the ancient Greek and Roman worlds and India. Many correspondences with Indian philosophy in the Upanishads have been found in the teachings of Pythagoras, Plato, Philo and Plotinus by scholars of comparative religion such as David Frawley. So the young Jesus could very well have become acquainted with Hindu, Buddhist and even Zoroastrian teachings without necessarily leaving home, but obviously not as thoroughly as he would have by visiting these lands for himself. The early Christian fathers also accepted the idea of reincarnation. The idea was so prevalent among Christian teachers that the Emperor Justinian had to denounce the teachings of Origen, the theologian who advocated this doctrine, at the Council of Constantinople in AD 553. No less an authority than Professor S Radhakrishnan, author of the standard two-volume work *A Source Book in Indian Philosophy*, reinforces this connection between Hinduism and Christianity. In his book *Eastern Religions and Western Thought* he makes the point that Jesus enlarges and transforms the Jewish conceptions in the light of his own personal experience. In this process he was helped considerably by his religious environment, which included Indian influences, as the tenets of the Essenes and the Book of Enoch show. In his teaching of the Kingdom of God, life eternal, ascetic emphasis, and even on the future life, he breaks away from Jewish tradition and approximates Hindu and Buddhist thought. Professor Radhakrishnan, later to become President of India, stated at the close of his masterly translation and commentary on *The Principal Upanishads*, that of the two pivotal sayings of Jesus – 'I and my Father are one', and 'Be ye perfect even as your Father which is in heaven is perfect' – the former falls into line with the spiritual idealism and non-dualistic doctrines of the Upanishads, the latter with the ethical idealism of Buddhism.

In the Katha Upanishad (I:3.14) we read: 'Arise, awake, having attained thy boons, understand them. Sharp as the edge of a razor and hard to cross, difficult to tread is that path, so Sages declare.' and in Matthew 7:14 we have a parallel saying from Jesus: 'Strive to enter in at the strait gate, for narrow is the gate and straightened the way that leads to life, and few be they that find it.' And we read in the Brhadaranyaka Upanishad: 'The narrow ancient path which stretches far away has been found by me. By it, the wise, the knowers of Brahman go up to the heavenly world after the fall of this body, being freed even while living.' This is parallel to John 14:6, where Christ simply proclaims, 'I am the way.' Again in the same Upanishad we read in III:5.1: 'Therefore let a Brahmana, after he has done with learning, desire to live as a child. When he has done both with the state of childhood and with learning, then he becomes a silent meditator. Having done with both the non-meditative and the meditative states, then he becomes a knower of

Brahman.' This is similar, if not parallel to Luke 10:21 and Matthew 18:3: 'In this hour Jesus rejoiced, saying, "I thank Thee, Heavenly Father, because Thou hast hidden these things from the wise and prudent and revealed them unto babes."' 'Except ye become like little children, ye shall not see the Kingdom of God.'

Thus a similar argument applies to Hinduism as with Buddhism. If he had visited India, Jesus would have come face to face with many enlightened Brahmin sages and rishis with whom India abounds, and this would undoubtedly influence his teaching. Again scholars have found many spiritual ideals which both teachings share in common. Their chief similarity focuses on the parallels found between the personality and teachings of Lord Krishna (who predates Christ) and Jesus Christ, also an incarnation of the Divine, and their similar message for humanity. Krishna's teachings, often in the form of beautiful poetic parables, aphorisms and metaphors are often very much like the recorded sayings of Jesus. The Bhagavad Gita and the New Testament contain innumerable teachings which both these divine incarnations hold in common. To mention a few, we have the affirmative injunction to love thy neighbour, be charitable to the poor and underprivileged, and to affirm perfect faith in the goodness, mercy and love of Almighty God. Evil must be confronted with love and forgiveness. Lusts of the flesh are condemned. The weak and the infirm are always to be supported. Work should be for the benefit of one's fellow man in a spirit of devotion. All forms of cruelty and tyranny are rigorously condemned. Salvation comes through both work and grace. Again, as with Buddhism, the principle of 'inwardness' is paramount. 'To seek the Kingdom of Heaven within' equals the Bhagavad Gita's emphasis on realization of the self, the

Godhood inherent in man, who is created in the divine image. Jesus, if and when he visited India, must have heard many insights from Hindu sages, which not only reinforced his faith in his native Judaism, but led to his greater emphasis on love, rather than law, as found in the Old Testament.

For many Hindus. Jesus is also the perfect embodiment of Dharma. Dharma may be loosely defined as 'the way of righteousness', but is best understood by its attributes, rather than any rigid definition. From a Hindu perspective Jesus exhibited all the attributes of a great Indian yogi. He possessed the *siddhas* (powers), as did the Buddha, such as walking on water, spiritual and bodily healing, and resuscitation from deep or deathlike trance states. Chaturvedi Bhadrinath, in his excellent book *Finding Jesus in Dharma*, states the attributes of Dharma very succinctly as follows, quoting from the great Indian epic the Mahabharata, in which the Bhagavad Gita appears. 'All the sayings of Dharma are with a view to nurturing, cherishing, providing more amply, enriching, prospering, increasing, enhancing, all living beings: in three words, securing their prabhava, or primordial essence, that is their original Self; their dharana, that is their powers of spiritual retention; and ahimsa, that is non-violence.' He continues, 'The meaning of Jesus is manifest in the truth, as he expressed it both in his life and in his teachings, that it is love, and not the law that nurtures, cherishes, enriches, enhances, brings together, sustains, supports, and brings freedom from fear and violence.' Jesus, from a Hindu point of view is therefore the embodiment of Dharma's attributes as well. Seen in this clear light, the meaning of Jesus is the meaning also of Hindu Dharma, of which, in his attributes he is a perfect embodiment.

Raimon Panikkar, the theologian, in his influential book *The Unknown Christ of Hinduism*, emphasizes that there are the common doctrines of salvation through grace and works in both Christianity and Hinduism. Many Christian missionaries also discovered that there was much in the higher forms of Hinduism, the Vedanta and Bhakti, that was akin to the Christian ideal of devotion. Both Hinduism and Christianity are religions of the 'Via Positiva', the affirmative way. The great Hindu sage, Sri Ramakrishna, demonstrated in action that self-realization was possible through Christianity as well as Hinduism. This was affirmed by his prominent disciple Vivekananda who recognized that both religions strive to realize the divine immanence which is inherent in every man and woman. 'The Kingdom of Heaven is within you,' (Luke 17:20–21) as Christ so forcibly stated. Like many an Indian sage, Jesus affirms that one can realize and attain that God-consciousness right here and now, everywhere and at all times. No message can be more enlightening or encouraging to the human heart than this!

Those who regard the possibility and probability of Jesus' visit to India and Tibet as more than a speculative hypothesis, lay great stress on these correspondences. To what extent they can be regarded as firm evidence of such a journey is controversial, but will be fully discussed in our concluding chapter. But first we must turn to that other great, higher world religion, Islam, and study its point of view on the whole question, which is revolutionary from a Christian standpoint, to say the least.

Chapter 7

The Islamic Point of View

Islam is a great higher religion whose contribution to the culture of the world in terms of architecture, philosophy and science has been considerable over the centuries. It has been a great civilizing influence in the Arab world. Although medieval in its laws, it aims at preserving a theocratic society for the faithful. Islam means submission to the will of God. It is a shame that a small minority of fundamentalist, violent extremists have proved so disturbing in recent times and led to conflict with the West. Islam is quite specific about Jesus, and I will endeavour to summarize their views. However, it is one particular sect of Islam, the Ahmadiyyas of Kashmir, which has the most to contribute on this whole vexatious question, as they are firmly convinced not only that did Jesus escape the crucifixion, as their sacred Koran states, but that he then went on to India, lived in Kashmir and was buried there after his death, in a tomb which can be visited today.

Briefly, orthodox Islam sees Isa (the Arabic form of his name) or Jesus as a great prophet of God sent to guide the children of Israel with a new scripture. Islam accepts the immaculate conception, which occurred by divine decree. Jesus was also granted the power to perform miracles, also by God. Most important for our investigation are the Koran's verses, which I shall quote as the chapter progresses, to the effect that Jesus was neither killed nor crucified, but raised up alive to heaven. He is destined to return to Earth before Judgement Day to restore the rule of righteousness and vanquish 'the false Messiah' or Antichrist. He is regarded as a Muslim in the sense that he taught surrender or submission to the divine will, the very foundation of the Moslem's faith. Islam rejects his special status as 'the son of God' but regards him as a prophet or messenger sent by God. The Koran contains many references to Jesus where he is sometimes referred to as al-Masih, the Messiah or anointed one; he is seen as a forerunner to their founder, the Prophet Mohammed.

The Islamic point of view is also supported by the discovery of the lost Gospel of Barnabas. The two known manuscripts of this text have been dated to the late-16th century and are written in Italian and Spanish respectively. There is also an early Syriac copy found near Hakkari in 1986. The gospel is also mentioned in two lists of apocryphal gospels in the 6th and 7th centuries respectively. The Barnabas Gospel is, however, disputed by Christian scholars, as are many of the Gnostic scriptures. It is approximately the same length as one of the canonical gospels. Some scholars believe that it is a remnant of an early apocryphal Gnostic gospel, but not to be confused with either the Gnostic Epistle of Barnabas, written in the 2nd century AD, or the Acts of Barnabas, written in Cyprus circa AD 430. This work bears strong parallels with the orthodox Islamic point of view, and even mentions Mohammad by name. Jesus is described as a prophet, not the son of God, and Paul is called the 'deceived'.

The gospel states that Jesus escaped crucifixion by being raised to heaven, similar to the prophet Elijah (2 Kings 2), while Judas Iscariot was crucified in his place. It does differ from the Koran in the respect that Jesus permits the drinking of wine. Most scholars seem to agree that, on stylistic grounds, there must have been a pre-existing heterodox text from which these copies were made. The gospel is distinctly anti-Pauline, and may have been written around the date of Paul's ministry. The work has been supported by respected Moslem thinkers such as the Egyptian Rashid Rida and Sayid Abul Ala Maududi in Pakistan, although it is not totally in accordance with Islamic tradition. The book's importance for Islam is that it categorically confirms the viewpoint of the Koran in stating that Jesus was never crucified as described in the canonical gospels.

The anglicized name of Jesus is derived from the Latin Iesus, which comes from the Greek Iesous. The Koranic references are to Isa, which is possibly y-sh, the Hebrew consonants of Yeshua having been reversed to give s-y, the Arabic consonants of isa. The name Isa assimilates with Musa (Moses), because they were sometimes paired. It also derives from the Syriac Yeshu, and Hebrew Yeshua (Joshua), coinciding remarkably accurately with the title of the Hemis Gospel of Issa discovered in Tibet, and where the term Musa, spelled as Mossa is also used for Moses. Notovitch appears not to have known about the Islamic point of view, so these coincidences could well be significant, but missed by him. The Ahmadiyyas use the name Yuz Asaf, which is most likely the Kashmiri version of Jesus son of Joseph, or a corruption of the Buddhist term Boddhisatva, which the Tibetans believed Jesus to have been.

The Ahmadiyya sect's point of view on this whole question

differs from orthodox Islam insofar as after his apparent death and resurrection he journeyed to Kashmir to teach the gospel, and lived in India for the remainder of his life. This belief is highly documented and well worth serious consideration. It is best stated in a book entitled *Jesus in India*, originally an Urdu treatise, written by the esteemed and saintly founder of the Ahmadiyya movement in Islam, Hadhrat Mirza Ghulam Ahmad of Qadian (1835–1908). The movement flourishes today, although it is regarded as heretical by the more orthodox Islamic authorities. There is substantial archaeological and literary evidence relating to his stay in India and his tomb in Kashmir which I shall describe more fully in this chapter.

In Islam, Jesus is revered as the last of the great prophets before Mohammad. In the Koran 5:76 there is a reference to the Messiah, the son of Mary, as a messenger; other messengers like him had gone before. Furthermore, the Koran clearly states that Jesus did not die on the Cross, and the Jews were deceived. In the Koran 4:156–7 it states: 'they did not kill him, nor did they crucify him, but he was made to appear as one crucified to them. Those that disagreed about him were in doubt about his death; what they knew about it was sheer conjecture ... in reality, God lifted him up to His Presence; He is mighty and wise.' Hadhrat Mirza Ghulam Ahmad's research furnishes the supporting evidence that in the Gnostic Gospel of Barnabas it is categorically denied that he died on the Cross. Further, Ahmad, in common with other Islamic scholars, believes that he deceived the Romans by feigning death, was then resuscitated and escaped from his tomb, where according to St Mark's Gospel, Chapter 16, 'he was later seen coming on the road to Galilee'. In verse 14 we read: 'he afterward appeared unto the eleven as they sat at meat.' To escape the Romans he then passed from Jerusalem through Nasibus and on to Iran through Afghanistan and then to Kashmir where he settled and eventually died, and was buried. According to Ahmad he also visited Tibet during his travels to India, and preached to the Buddhist monks, confirming both Dowling's and Notovitch's theses.

Ahmad argues that a significant passage in the gospels seems to point to the fact that he escaped the Crucifixion, which was not an impossibility, as I will show in chapter 9. In Matthew 12 verse 40 Jesus says: 'For as Jonas was three days and three nights in the whale's belly; so shall the son of man be three days and three nights in the heart of the earth.' The implication was that after three days in the tomb, he would emerge fully alive, to take part in life again. Furthermore, in Luke 24 verses 28–30 we read: 'and they drew nigh unto the village whither they went; and he made as though he would have gone further. But they constrained him, saying, "Abide with us; for it is toward evening and the day is far spent," and he went to tarry with them. And it came to pass, as he sat at meat with them, he took bread, and blessed it, and broke, and gave to them.' Ahmad and others have interpreted this as meaning he was very much alive. Spirits have no need to sit down to eat meat and bread; these are the actions of a living man.

This view is strongly reinforced by Luke 24 verse 39 where he says, 'Behold my hands and my feet, that it is I myself, handle me and see for a spirit hath not flesh and bones as ye see me have', It was if he was proving to them he was alive as flesh and blood and not a spirit. In verse 40 we read: 'And when he had thus spoken, he showed them his hands and his feet.' Then in verse 41 we read: 'And while they yet believed not for joy and wonder, he said unto them, "Have ye any meat?"' Verse 42 says: 'And they gave him a piece of a broiled fish and an honey comb.' In verse 43 the narrative continues: 'And he took it and did eat before them.' All these verses tend to confirm the Islamic standpoint that Jesus was very much alive and not a spirit, and went so far as to prove to his disciples that he had indeed escaped the Crucifixion. Dr Holger Kersten makes the cogent point that some modern authorities in Eastern religions are of the opinion that the real truth about Jesus and his life was much better preserved by early Islam rather than by the early Christians. Mohammad may well have determined to protect the original teachings of Jesus against the many later ecclesiastical distortions about his death and his message. The holy Koran, also a divinely revealed scripture, is absolutely unequivocal in saying 'they did not kill him nor did they crucify him'.

According to Ahmad and other Islamic authorities, Jesus decided to take refuge from further Roman persecution in Kashmir because it was believed at that time that certain lost tribes of Israel had settled there, and Jesus would have felt very much at home amongst his own people, and warmly welcomed. There were ten tribes of the Israelites, who 721 years before Christ had been taken prisoner from Samaria by Shalmaneser, King of Assur, and taken away by him. Ultimately some of these tribes were dispersed and some came to settle in India.

Around 35 miles to the southeast of Srinigar near Bijbihara is the Aish-Muquam cave (Aish derives from Issa or Isha and Muquam means a place of rest), at the entrance to which an impressive shrine has been built to house the tomb of the famous 15th-century Islamic Saint Zainuddin Wali. This saint owned a staff that had been presented to him by the famous Sheikh Noodr Din Wali. The staff is housed inside the shrine. This olive-wood staff is over 2 metres in length and 25 millimetres thick, and is known as the Rod of Jesus; it was believed to have been used by him when living in Kashmir.

There is literary evidence in the *Rajah Tarangini*, a history of Kashmir by the 12th-century poet, Pandit Kalhana. It tells of the holy man Isana, who performed many miracles there. It is believed that this Isana refers to none other than Issa or Jesus.

This is confirmed by the 10th-century historian Sheikh Al-Said-us-Sadiq, in his renowned work *Ikmal-ud-Din*, translated by no less a person than Oxford professor, Dr Max Muller, to whom we have referred previously as editor of the 50-volume *Sacred Books Of the East*. Muller, although a sceptic, translated this book from a copy published in Iran in 1883, telling of the journey of Jesus to India and his death in Kashmir as Yuz Asaf. The link between the name Yuz Asaf and Jesus is discussed further in this chapter. This book contains the same parable of the 'Farmer Who Goes Forth To Sow Seeds' as is found in the canonical gospels. Also, the Arabic version of the 'Story of Barlaam and Joasaph' (The Book of Balauer and Budasef) tells of the death of Yuz Asaf in Kashmir, when he was believed to have been 80 years old. Incidentally, in this book, especially in the Arabic and Hebrew versions, we find a number of fables, many of which derive from Indian sources. Dr Hugh Schonfield, in his absorbing book *The Essene Odyssey*, writes that in 'Barlaam and Joasaph' we even find Barachias as the name of a Christian who came to the assistance of Joasaph and ultimately succeeded him as King of the Indian State. In the Christian version, this Joasaph is a disciple of Jesus, and there is an attempt to identify the mysterious prophet Joasaph with Jesus or, as he is known in Kashmir, Yuz Asaph.

The most important evidence of all, however, is found in the centre of Srinigar's old town, Anzimar. Here lies the tomb of Yuz Asaf, the name for Jesus which coincides with an inscription found on the throne of Solomon, at the time when Solomon's Temple was later restored by the Persians. According to the historian Mullah Nadiri in his *History of Kashmir* (1413) we read: 'At this time, Yuz Asaf announced his prophetic mission, in the year fifty and four. He is Jesus, prophet of the sons of Israel.' Nadiri continues to write: 'At the time of Gopadatta's reign, Yuz Asaf came up from the Holy land into this valley (Kashmir), and announced he was a prophet. He epitomised the peak of piety and virtue, and proclaimed that he was himself his own message, that he dwelled in God, night and day, and that he had made God known to the people of Kashmir ... I have also read in a Hindu book that this prophet is really Hazrat Issa (Arabic for the revered Jesus), the Spirit of God, and he adopted the name Yuz Asaf. This name is probably entomologically derived from Bodhisattva, when Kashmir was Buddhist and Hindu before the arrival of Islam. After his death, his body was buried in Mohalla Anzimarrah (Anzimar in Srinigar).' (Extract from the *Tarikh-i-Kashmir* page 69)

The building constructed around this tomb is called the Rozabel (the tomb of noble or saintly ones). Above the entrance to the burial chamber is an inscription which states that Yuz Asaf entered Kashmir many hundreds of years ago, dedicated to bringing his message of Truth. The sarcophagus containing his remains is aligned east–west according to the Orthodox Jewish tradition. All the substantial references to Jesus having spent his later years in Kashmir are reinforced by the considerable folk memory as in Tibet, over 2,000 years, which is generally, if not invariably, founded on known events, engraved in the people's collective traditions. So it is a reasonable assumption, by the many proponents of this thesis, that the body of Jesus does indeed lie buried in the Rozabel at Srinigar.

In addition, near the tomb of Yuz Asaf there is another temple on Mount Solomon, known as Takht-i-Sulamain. It is claimed that this was an exact replica of the building outside Jerusalem commonly known as the Tomb of Absolom, and confirms the Hebrew presence in Kashmir from an early date.

Many ancient literary works in Kashmir testify to the fact that Yuz Asaf and Jesus are one and the same. One old manuscript (according to M Yasin, in his book *Mysteries of Kashmir* 1972) describes the shrine as the grave of Issa Rooh-Allah (Jesus, Spirit of God, the Holy Spirit). It was also the practice of worshippers to place memorial candles around the tombstones. When the centuries-old layers of wax were removed, the sensational discovery was made of a pair of footprints carved into the stone. This was a widespread tradition at the shrines of saints. Beside these footprints there lay a crucifix and a rosary. The relief of Yuz Asaf's footprints shows an umistakeable mark of identification – the scars of the Crucifixion wounds. The left foot had even been nailed over the right according to Roman custom. In 1776 the Grand Mufti of Islam, Rahman Mir (Teacher of Islamic Religious Law), issued a formal decree, The Seal of the Justice of Islam-Mulla Fazil, in The High Court of Justice, in the Department of Learning and Piety of the Kingdom to the effect that 'Here lies Yuz Asaf, who came as a prophet to Kashmir. He ministered to the people, declared his unity with God, and was a lawgiver to the people. Since then his tomb has been honoured by kings, state officials, high dignitaries and the common folk.' (Kersten, page 230) All this cumulative evidence seems to point to the supposition that Jesus may very well have come to Kashmir after escaping death from the Crucifixion. The tomb has never been opened to this day, because of the considerable risk of extremist civil and terrorist disturbances in Kashmir, especially due to the territorial dispute that exists there between India and Pakistan.

The following manuscripts support the Islamic point of view.

THE HOLY KORAN

[3:55] And when Allah said: O Isa [Jesus] I am going to terminate the period of your stay on earth and cause you to ascend unto Me and purify you of those who disbelieve and make those who follow you above those who disbelieve to the day of resurrection; then to Me shall be your return, so I will decide between you concerning that in which you differed.

[4:155–9] Then because of their breaking of their covenant, and their disbelieving in the revelations of Allah, and their slaying of the prophets wrongfully, and their saying: 'Our hearts are hardened-Nay', but Allah set a seal upon them for their disbelief, so that they believe not save a few – And because of their disbelief and of their speaking against Mary a tremendous calumny: And because of their saying: 'We slew the Messiah, Jesus son of Mary, Allah's messenger' –

they slew him not nor crucified him, but it appeared so unto them; and lo! Those who disagree concerning it are in doubt thereof; they have no knowledge save pursuit of a conjecture; they slew him not for certain. But Allah took him up unto Himself. Allah was ever Mighty, Wise. There is not one of the People of the Scripture but will believe in him before his death, and on the Day of Resurrection he will be a witness against them.

[4:171] O followers of the Book! [The Bible] do not exceed the limits of your religion, and do not speak lies against Allah, but speak the Truth; the Messiah, Isa son of Marium [Jesus son of Mary] is only an apostle of Allah and His Word which he communicated to Marium and a spirit from Him; believe therefore in Allah and His apostles, and say not, Three. Desist, it is better for you; Allah is only one God; far be It from His glory that He should have a son, whatever is in the heavens and whatever is in the earth is His, and Allah is sufficient for a Protector.

[61:6] And when Isa son of Marium said: 'O children of Israel surely I am the apostle of Allah to you, verifying that which is before me of the Taurat [Torah] and giving the good news of an Apostle who will come after me, his name being Ahmad [Mohammad],' but when he came to them with clear arguments they said: 'This is clear magic.'

The *Rauza Tus-Safa* contains biographies of the prophets, kings and caliphs, in seven volumes, written by Mir Mohammad in AD 1417. It tells of the journey of Jesus from Jerusalem to India.

The *Tarikh-i-Kashmir* is a renowned work by Mullah Nadiri,

the first Kashmiri historian. It tells of the events leading to Jesus' declaration of his ministry in Kashmir. For example: 'During this time Hazrat Yuz-Asaph, having travelled from the Land of Israel and entered this Holy Valley of Kashmir, proclaimed his prophethood. He devoted his days and nights in prayer, and having reached the higher realms of spiritual virtue, announced himself as a prophet for Kashmir. I have noted in a Hindu scripture that this prophet was really Hazrat Issa, the Spirit of God, who took the name of Yuz Asaph in Kashmir. He spent the remainder of his life in this valley and after his death was entombed in Anzimar, Srinigar. It is known that the aura of prophethood emanates from this tomb.'

The Kamal-Ud-Din tells of the first journey of Jesus to India, from Hindu sources. It gives many parables addressed to the Kashmiri people and also mentions his later visit, and the presence of the Apostle Thomas in Kashmir for the burial of Jesus. The book was written in Persian by the historian Al-Thaik Sadiq ALi-Jafar, who died in AD 912. Western scholars have found this book to be of great value. It was first printed in Iran in 1881 and translated by the sceptical professor Dr Max Muller of Heidelberg and Oxford Universities into German.

The Tarikh-I-Azami is written by Khawaja Muhammad Azam Dedmari, one of the most famous Kashmir historians. This book was written in AD 1827, and refers to Jesus' burial place in Kashmir. Finally, the impressive Islamic standpoint is considerably reinforced by the life work of Professor Fida Hassnain of the University of Kashmir in Srinigar. Dr Hassnain is still alive, as I write, and is highly respected as an Islamic scholar of international repute. He has written several well-regarded books, and has been a visiting professor in Japan and the United States to different universities. He is the Director of the Kashmir Research Centre for Buddhist Studies, and was a member of the International Conference for Anthropological Research in Chicago. Until his retirement in 1985 he was also the Executive Director of all the museums, collections and archives in Kashmir, based at the Ministry of Culture. Over the last 25 years he has gathered a wealth of facts, implications, associations and apparent connections to prove that Jesus once lived and worked in Kashmir. Dr Holger Kersten visited Professor Hassnain in Kashmir, but believes all his researches still need to be put on an exact and firmer scientific footing before they can prove the case conclusively, and finally put the whole issue beyond any shadow of a doubt. However, those that believe in the Jesus in Kashmir legend will find ample, well-argued, well-documented research material to support their case, and much of what I have written is drawn from this resource.

A very interesting discovery which supports the Islamic point of view is found in the travels of the explorer, O M Burke, who reported in his travel book *Among The Dervishes* that he encountered a Muslim sect (the Ahmadiyya) claiming to be followers of Jesus, identified with Yuz Asaf the Kashmiri. They were in possession of a holy book quite distinct from the gospels and entitled 'Tradition of the Messiah'. In what Burke reports of the sect's teaching there was an admixture of elements from various religions, including relics of Essene and Nazorean concepts. It is only fair to point out, however, that according to the *Encyclopaedia of Islam*, the Ahmadiyya point of view is considered to be partly heretical, insofar as it does not accord precisely with the account of Jesus' death in the Koran.

Nevertheless, to support the Ahmadiyya's point of view, in addition to the weighty authority of the Koran, that he was never crucified, we have the literary and archaeological evidence reinforced by 2,000 years of folk memory that he took refuge in Kashmir, after escaping from death on the Cross. In our concluding Chapter we shall discuss the merits of this case in more detail.

Chapter 8

The Problem of the Missing Years

Before we review all the evidence for and against the proposition that Jesus visited India and Tibet in his 'missing years', we must examine the other possibilities of how he might have spent his time from the age of 12, when he discoursed with the learned rabbis in the Temple, to when he commenced his ministry, and his baptism by John, at the age of 30. The gospels are completely silent on this whole question for some inexplicably unknown reason. It is one of the great historical mysteries of all time: how did Jesus spend those 18 to 19 years, and why are all the four Evangelists completely silent on the matter? This has led to endless speculation as to what he might have done, and we will review some of the main suggestions, before we consider that most challenging and sensational theory, that he visited India and Tibet.

These 'missing years' are sometimes called the 'hidden years' or the 'lost years', the 'concealed years' or the 'secret years', because his disappearance was never revealed by the early Church for unknown reasons of their own. If, as many have suggested, he retired into an Essene Community, then because of the Essenes' link with Orthodox Judaism, it might have been politic to keep silent, in a Pauline early Church determined to distance itself from traditional Judaism, and to be the new world religion for the Gentiles. The Essene theory is quite possible, however, because Jesus' teaching and his asceticism have many parallels. These we will examine in more detail. A more monastic order to which he may have been attracted was the Theraputae, and although they were not considered to be as orthodox in their Judaism as the Essenes, it also may have been felt prudent by the early Church not to disclose such a link. Then there is the fairly simple theory that he merely worked with his father as a carpenter, and remained with his family in Jerusalem. This sounds too ordinary and commonplace for such a dynamic, spiritual personality, as his considerable powers would have developed in his adolescent years until he reached manhood. It has also been suggested that the gospels deliberately kept silent, as a literary device, quickly to come to the important period of his life, his actual ministry and crucifixion. There is also some far-fetched speculation that the wealthy Joseph of Arimathea patronized Jesus and took the young boy on journeys around the known world. According to some visionaries, this would even have included Great Britain, with a visit to Glastonbury. This fanciful idea is held by no less a notable personage than the great English mystic William Blake, who wrote in his popular poem 'Jerusalem', 'And did those feet in ancient time walk upon England's mountain green?' This idea has led to endless speculations, and it is best to return to the more reasonable probabilities. Let us first look at the Essene hypotheses.

The Essenes

The Essenes were an important, revered, Jewish ascetic community that flourished between the 2nd century BC and the 1st century AD alongside the Pharisees and the Sadducees. There is considerable information written about them by the influential and highly reliable Jewish mystic, philosopher, judiciary and Gnostic, Philo of Alexandria, a contemporary of Jesus, but surprisingly never mentioned by him. There was also the major discovery of the Dead Sea Scrolls in 1946, which unveiled to the world the Essene redaction of the Old Testament scriptures, and their different spiritual texts.

In two important surviving works by Philo, *Every Good Man Is Free* and the *Hypothetica*, we have considerable information about the Essenes which illustrate a way of life which may very well have appealed to the youthful, spiritually prodigious Yeshua (Joshua), the son of Joseph, later to be translated by the Greeks as Jesus, used by the Romans, and then called by the Greeks, for Saviour, as The Christ. Philo estimated that there were approximately 4,000 Essenes among the Jewish community in and around Jerusalem. He believed the name derived from an inexact form of the Greek meaning 'holiness'. They were devoutly pious, and abstained from animal sacrifice, resolving, above all, to sanctify their minds. They avoided the cities and denounced slavery, upholding the equality and brotherhood of man. Their interest in money was only to maintain life's necessities. They toiled on the land and engaged only in the crafts necessary for their well-being. They dwelled in communities, and their doors were always open to one another. They held a single treasury, took meals in common, and any sick and aged were cared for by them. They did not marry, and pursued a life of celibacy, comparable to the later Christian monastic way of life. Newly joined members vowed an oath of loyalty towards the One God of Israel, and to practise righteousness in all their dealings. They were permitted to join the community from the age of 11, so Jesus, at 12, would have been eligible. He could also have received Bar Mitzvah, an initiation into manhood at the age of 13, with them. Their theology included faith in the soul's immortality, which would be restored after death. Their rituals consisted of purification by bathing. They did not eat meat. Many scholars believe they were influenced by the mystical Greek sect, the Pythagoreans. John the Baptist is also regarded as a prime example of an Essene. It is easy to imagine that living in an Essene community would prove very attractive indeed to the young Jesus; perhaps much more fulfilling than merely practising carpentry. Here the mysteries of the esoteric doctrines of the Kabbalah transmitted by Menachem and Nehunya Ben Ha-Kanah would have been discussed and revealed. He would have been free to grow up and mature in an intensely spiritual and religious environment. He could have exchanged views with devoutly pious men. Many scholars have noted that the similarities in many respects between Christianity and the Essenes are striking. There was the same communism, belief in ritual bathing or baptism, the power of prophecy, aversion to marriage, belief in a Messianic advent, and a similar system of organization; as well as the same rules for travellers dedicated to charitable work, and the enjoyment of communal meals. We may well ask, if this was the case, why, if the young Jesus grew up to manhood as an Essene, as was definitely possible if not probable, was it never disclosed in the gospels? The general view is that the early Pauline Church was anxious to distance itself from Orthodox Judaism, and propagate a world religion easily accessible to the Gentiles, without the burden of circumcision and other strict Talmudic and Halachic injunctions. This would explain the silence of the four synoptic gospels about the missing years, especially chosen from many available gospels, to be the final canon of Christian scriptural authority. In an interesting book *The Lost Years of Jesus Revealed*, written by the scholarly Anglican Reverend Dr Charles Francis Potter after the discovery of the Dead Sea Scrolls, the learned author writes: 'one thing is emerging from the study of the Scrolls – namely, that the beliefs, teachings and practices of Jesus himself, although not identical in all respects with those of the Essene schools that he probably attended during the "silent years", were apparently closer to those of the Essenes than to those of the bishops of the Ecumenical Council which determined the Nicene Creed of Orthodox Christianity.'

The Therapeutae

The Therapeutae, also a Jewish ascetic community, claimed to possess a unique art of healing, and this is the reason why the word 'therapeutic' has become so widespread in our language. Philo, in his treatise entitled *The Contemplative Life*, makes the distinction between them and the Essenes who, in his opinion, followed a more active life than the Therapeutae, who were more contemplative in their disposition. Their most essential characteristic was their mystical aspiration to reach the vision and unification with the One God. They renounced private property, so they could gain leisure for the contemplative life. They freed themselves from family cares and ties, avoiding the cities and seeking solitude in country villages. They set aside a room for prayer, the study of scripture and the composition of hymns. They visited the Synagogue on Sabbath. They only ate one meal per day, at sunset, and were known to fast for three whole days or more. Their diet was mainly bread and water. The elders gave discourses to the other members. They permitted chaste women to be members and formed mixed choirs.

An interesting suggestion which may have some relevance to the Buddhist influences on early Christianity is the novel research by Zacharias P Thundy, a respected specialist in the application of linguistics to religion. He claims that the word 'therapeutae' is itself of Buddhist origin. He believes it to be a Hellenization of the Sanskrit/Pali term 'theravada', which was the name of the Buddhist school whose members set off from Gandhara to the West, as decided by the Council of Asoka.

Philo actually states that their sacred laws had schooled them to worship the 'Self-Existent'. This is a very advanced spiritual practice, focused on the immanence of God, rather than only on His external transcendence. Did not Jesus say, 'The Kingdom of Heaven is within you'? Such a dictum would coincide with the Therapeutae's worship of the Self-Existent, akin to the Hindu concept of self-realization, or the Athenian Socratic injunction to 'Know Thy Self'. Incidentally, Philo also claims that Moses worshipped the 'Self-Existent' in section VII of *Every Good Man Is Free*. It is interesting to ponder on the revelation by God to Moses, when He stated categorically that His name was 'I Am That I Am' from the burning bush, as this is also a Vedantic formulation. Philo writes: 'who among those who profess piety deserve to be compared with these (the Therapeutae) ... they keep the memory of God alive and never forget it.' They also interpreted the scriptures allegorically rather than literally. Again, it is very easy to imagine that the young Jesus could well have been very happy, living among the Theraputae during his 'hidden years'. Unless, of course, he had an even greater ambition, to learn the wisdom of the Far East, in India and Tibet, as a foundation for his ministry. That is the burning question which this book raises for every reader's serious consideration.

The Gnostics

One of the favoured solutions to the problem of the 'missing years' was the possibility that Jesus spent time with different spiritual groups. In addition to the Essenes and the Therapeutae, there were the Gnostics. The title 'Gnostics' was derived from the Greek 'gnosis' meaning knowledge. The gnosis that this sect was interested in finding was direct, experiential, immanent knowledge of God. They had studied the Hermetic wisdom of ancient Egypt, a mystical and cosmological system which placed emphasis on the immanence of the Divine in each soul, and a transcendent power which governed the universe through a hierarchy of archangels, angels, and archetypal forces engaged in a struggle between 'darkness' and 'light'. These powers were often given biblical names or new names derived from the Greek language. After the death of Jesus numerous Gnostic gospels appeared under the authorship of the different Apostles, such as James, Thomas, Peter, Philip, Judas and even Mary Magdalene. These give a totally different picture of Jesus from the canonical gospels, and portray him principally as a great revealer of cosmic mysteries. In the Nag Hammadi Egyptian desert discoveries of 1947, over 50

Gnostic gospels were found. The early Church Fathers had condemned them all as heretical, and proclaimed the four canonical gospels as the only true record. But if these somewhat sanitized synoptic gospels did not really represent the true Gnostic Jesus, and wished to dismiss his 19 years of youth, adolescence and early manhood, in silence, then during the 'missing years' the prodigious Jesus could well have spent his time secretly studying these ancient mysteries before commencing his great mission. This is, however, only supposition, and is not grounded on any evidence, except for the appearance of so many Gnostic gospels, attributed to Apostles, after his demise, all claiming to proclaim the real Jesus. This is an extensive topic of discussion and I would refer the interested reader to my own books *The Essential Gnostic Gospels* and *The Gnostic Gospels* for renditions of these ancient texts, to discover for himself another portrayal of Jesus, quite different from what we have been conditioned to believe simply by reading Matthew, Mark, Luke and John.

A most novel and unique interpretation of 'the missing years' is provided by the active American-based Urantia Foundation. The Urantia Foundation published the *Urantia Book*, a spiritual and philosophical work which originated sometime between 1925 and 1955. This book was revealed through an anonymous spiritual medium and given to his medical practitioner, Dr William Sadler, who later became the publisher. The comments which apply to the whole question of the validity of spiritual mediumship and channelling, will be discussed in the final chapter of this book. Their hypotheses have been dealt with exhaustively by Douglas Mayberry, a prolific author for the

Urantia Foundation, in his book *Jesus: The Missing Years*. In this novel biography of Christ it suggests that in his 'missing years', at the age of 28, Jesus 'met a wealthy traveller and his son, a young man of about 17 years of age. These travellers hailed from India, being on their way to visit Rome and various other points on the Mediterranean ... the father was insistent that Jesus consent to travel with them ... Jesus agreed to make the trip.' It is interesting that this almost archetypal fascination with an Indian connection and Jesus crops up again and again, although in a totally different form. In fact, in Mayberry's book, Jesus does not go to India with his Indian mentors but visits Joppa, Caesarea, Alexandria, Crete, Carthage, Naples, Rome, Corinth, Athens, Ephesus, Antioch, Mesopotamia and the Caspian. He gives many discourses at each port of call. The whole book is 300 pages in length, and it is not possible to summarize its history and content any further, as it does not take Jesus to India and Tibet, the object of our enquiry. It is sufficient to add that the book deals with Jesus' childhood and education in Palestine in a conventional way, as does Alfred Reynolds in his novel *The Hidden Jesus*, and the Israeli Sholem Asch in his celebrated novel *The Nazarene*. The controversial *Urantia Book* has never achieved anything approaching the fame or influence of the 'Aquarian Gospels', but is at the same time a novel and relevant addition to the large literature on this intriguing mystery for those who wish to read and explore every possibility.

Yet another book, *The Autobiography of Jesus of Nazareth and the Missing Years* by Richard G Patton, is also influenced by channelling. The author claims that under past-life regression therapy he discovered that he was in some form or other familiar with Jesus in Jerusalem, in a past life, and was able to relate an account of his missing years. The consequence is a narrative which broadly follows the events in India and Tibet as set down in Notovitch's Gospel of Issa. However, this book could be seen as a confirmation of the Gospel of Issa, or as a book written by someone who had come across it and was under its influence.

An interesting but little known book which confirms both Dowling's and Notovitch's affirmation that Jesus visited India and Tibet is *Fragments of The Hidden Years of Jesus* by 'The Scribe'. Like Levi Dowling's now famous Aquarian Gospel, the little known *Fragments* was channelled – in the author's words, 'given to me from "the other side"' – during many sittings with a famous medium, Mrs Gradon-Thomas, who was always in the very deepest trance. A spirit calling himself 'The Messenger' controlled her and dictated to The Scribe directly. Neither the medium nor The Scribe could have written this book, and his responsibility is confined to the transcription of the subject matter. The Scribe is anonymous, although the British Library copy is inscribed with the letter 'K' in pencil. It was written especially for members of the Great White Brotherhood. The Messenger is the high spirit who dictated the book. Chapter four of this 80-page book is titled 'Jesus in Tibet' and chapter six is called 'Jesus in India'. Other chapters describe Jesus in Egypt and Persia. In the Tibetan chapter we enter a monastery where there are members of the Great White Brotherhood. The Great White Brotherhood has been influential in very many Theosophical and New Age organizations, and is a group of supernatural beings of great power guiding humanity from 'the other side'. They are also called the Great Brotherhood of Light, a spiritual hierarchy composed of those ascended masters who have risen from the earth into immortality, but still maintain active watch over the world. The idea has been prevalent in esoteric circles since the 18th century and developed by the Theosophical movement under Madame Blavatsky. In this book, one of them, named Martreb, relates: 'that Jesus between the ages of twelve and thirty retired to a quiet place like this, to seek knowledge and instruction … how many people are there on your earth plane who think that during those years of which you have little or no record, Jesus was doing carpentry in his father's shop? They do not realize that he was spending his time with the great masters of Wisdom on both sides of the veil.' The cell that Jesus retired into was at the top of a great monastery on one of the highest mountains in Tibet, where he received lessons from a master. In the monastery, under instruction, he was given the first realization of the Cross and the way that led to his mission, and the events that would take place. When Jesus eventually leaves Tibet he moves to India, led by an angel, where in a temple he is instructed by a doctor of the law in the ancient Indian mysteries and Eastern esoteric wisdom. The book contains many descriptions of the monastery and temple interiors, and tells how Jesus entered deep meditation there, where he was given guidance necessary for his great forthcoming ministry on Earth, and its future. Although this book confirms the Indian and Tibetan hypotheses, its details differ considerably from both Dowling and Notovitch. Like all channelled revelations it is subject to the same possible criticisms that apply to The Aquarian Gospel which I summarize in chapter 10, Summary and Conclusions.

One of the questions often raised by sceptics is: how could

Jesus possibly travel in those early days on such a long and arduous journey; and what route would he have taken? Both the Aquarian and Issa gospels suggest he travelled with merchants. This was indeed possible because the famous Silk Route connecting all the regions of Asia with the east and west was widely used by merchants, pilgrims, monks, soldiers, nomads and urban dwellers from all over Asia. This overland route had been in use for at least a century before the birth of Jesus, and had been initiated by the Han Dynasty, to interconnect different trade routes. No doubt these merchants travelled in caravan with appropriate vehicles, and either camels, horses or mules – whichever were best suited for the terrain. The merchants did a thriving trade in luxuries such as silk, satins, musk, rubies, spices, diamonds and pearls between China, India and Asia Minor and the Mediterranean. Jesus' possible route, according to Islamic sources, could have been from Jerusalem, through Mosul, Tehran, Herat, Kabul, Peshawar and then on to Srinigar. Jesus would have been comfortable and well looked after by the merchants. Certain Islamic and Gnostic sources suggest that he was accompanied by Mary Magdalene, Mary his Mother and Mary his sister. Many may think that this enters the sphere of romantic fancy, as folk legend is often embroidered with details to appeal to the popular imagination so as to remain in the memory. But as myth and legend are invariably rooted in some fact or other, it does not affect their validity. However, some pottery with Tamil Brahmi inscriptions was found in 1995 at Berenike, a Roman settlement on the Red Sea coast of Egypt. These discoveries provided some material evidence to corroborate the literary accounts of a flourishing mercantile trade between India and the Roman Empire, of which Jerusalem was a provincial outpost.

The belief that some Jews originated from India was very prevalent in ancient Rome. In his book *The Lost Tribes*, Dr George Moore, a famous explorer and archaeologist, wrote that he had found many Hebrew inscriptions on sites in India. Quite close to Taxila, now in Sirkap, Pakistan, a stone was excavated that bears an inscription in Aramaic. The 11th-century Arab historian Biruni has written that in his own time no foreigners were being permitted to enter Kashmir other than Hebrews. Many Kashmiris, to this day, believe that they were descended from one of the Lost Tribes owing to their very obvious Semitic appearance and certain similar ritual customs.

In his famous *History of the Jews*, Flavius Josephus (AD 37–100) recorded that no less a person than the great Greek philosopher Aristotle had said that the Jews were derived from the Indian philosophers, and called by the Indians Calani. The same view was echoed by the historian Clearchus of Soli, and by Megasthenes, Alexander the Great's literary Ambassador to India. According to Dr Fida Hassnain, Emperor Claudius is reputed to have found an ancient scroll of the Torah in Kashmir, which was written on leather and was 48 feet in length when unrolled. Even to this day the Jews are known by many Indians as 'The Brahmins of the West'.

The Book of Genesis indicates that Abraham's first home was in Haran. There is a town in northern India called Haran, a few miles north of Srinigar, capital of Kashmir. From Haran, Abraham may have journeyed to Ur and then on to Canaan. Many people have pondered on the coincidence of the name Abraham being almost a complete anagram of 'A Brahman'. There is even a group of Israeli academics who have authored an impressive book called *Torah and Veda*, pointing out the many similarities between Judaism and the ancient Vedic religion. That Jesus was observed in India is further confirmed by the ninth volume of the Bhavishyat Maha Purana, which I paraphrased in the previous chapter. Dr Kersten points out that well over 300 of the names of geographical features of towns, regions and estates, and of tribes, clans, families and individuals in the Old Testament can be matched with linguistically related or phonetically similar names in Kashmir and its environs. Andreas Faber Kaiser, an investigative journalist who thoroughly researched the 'Jesus went to India' hypothesis and wrote a book entitled *Jesus Died in India*, also visited Tibet and Kashmir. Like Kersten, he came to similar conclusions and published a list of similar Kashmiri names correlating with places in Israel. Recently, as I write, the Israeli government has resolved to allow the remaining 7,232 members of the Bnei Menashe Jewish Community in India to immigrate to Israel. The Bnei Menashe claim descent from the lost tribe of Menashe, one of the lost ten tribes exiled by the Assyrians over 2,700 years ago.

In 1845 the missionary doctor Joseph Wolff reported in his book *Narrative of a Mission to Bokhara* that there were 10,000 Jews there. Today the Jews of Cochin are well known, and there is still a practising Jewish community with an active synagogue. So the supposition that there were also Jews settled in Kashmir is not at all far fetched, and is a very good explanation as to why, when Jesus sought refuge from the vengeful Romans, he escaped to distant Kashmir. There he would feel at home and could bring his mission to the lost Jews of Israel.

There is still further archaeological evidence that Jesus visited India provided by a grave, discovered by the explorer and much admired academic artist Nicholas Roerich, who found a tomb north of Ladakh, near Kashgar in 1930. This is described in his illustrated book The *Heart Of Asia*. It is believed, in the local oral tradition handed down from generation to generation, that this grave is definitely that of a certain Mary who travelled with Jesus to India, Tibet and Kashmir. The Gnostic Gospel of Philip mentions three women who remained with Jesus after his survival from the cross. Coincidently all three were named Mary, his mother, his sister and the Magdalene.

Chapter 9

The Crucifixion and Resurrection Mysteries

An essential part of the Islamic point of view depends on the Koranic verses which say that Jesus escaped the Crucifixion. This is not a suggestion unheard of in Christian and scholarly circles, radical as it may seem.

Dr Hugh Schonfield, author of the one-time bestselling scholarly book, *The Passover Plot*, makes the cogent point that from a medical standpoint it was possible to survive this ordeal. First-hand information about this is furnished by the Roman historian Josephus. In his autobiography, he writes that during the final stage of the siege of Jerusalem by the Roman legions, Titus had sent him to inspect a potential camp site at Tekoa, 12 miles due south of Jerusalem. On his return he passed a number of crucified prisoners, three of whom were friends. When he returned, he pleaded to Titus for their release. Titus relented, and ordered the three to be taken down and resuscitated. Two of them died, but one recovered and survived.

In Jesus' case his ordeal only lasted three hours, according to St John's Gospel. Private arrangements for his escape could well

THE CRUCIFIXION AND RESURRECTION MYSTERIES

have been made by his trusted friend Joseph of Arimathea, a wealthy man and member of the Sanhedrin, a Messiah-minded Pharisee, favoured by the Romans. Dr Schonfield suggests in another book, *The Essene Odyssey*, that there could well have been a plan to preserve Jesus through the agency of Joseph of Arimathea and his associates, a possibility which the gospel accounts would permit. Because of his influential status Joseph was able to obtain permission from Pontius Pilate to immediately receive the unconscious body of Jesus before sunset on the day of the Crucifixion. Spices and clean linen had been brought which would be antiseptic and help to staunch the wounds, and Jesus was immediately conveyed to a nearby tomb which was above ground and ventilated. The opened entrance of the tomb, the missing body and the discarded wrappings could mean that an attempt was made to rescue the living Jesus. The one or more men dressed in white seen by the women who came to perform the offices for the dead could have been Essenes, who wore this garb, who were friends of Joseph, rather than angels. Their presence would tend to support the possibility that Jesus' rescue and recovery was planned, since the Essenes, like the Theraputae, were highly skilled in the healing arts. If this was indeed the case the words of the most faithful Mary Magdalene would ring true when she told Peter, 'They have taken the Master out of the sepulchre and we do not know where they have placed him.' (John 20:2)

Hadhrat Mirza Ghulam Ahmad of Qadian believed that the wounds of Jesus would have healed in a few days. This is because of a certain salve, referred to in many ancient medical texts, called the Marham-i-Isa or the Ointment of Jesus. John's Gospel confirmed that the body had been wound in a linen cloth in which spices had been laid in the folds (John 11:44, 19:40).

The story in John's Gospel implies that the Roman soldiers were surprised to see that Jesus appeared to be dead so soon. As Dr Roger James has pointed out in published correspondence in *The London Review of Books* on this point: 'with the effusion pressing on his heart and body and his body fixed upright, he would probably have gone into severe heart failure, and would have appeared dead even though his heart was perfectly sound. The spear blow that was expected to finish him off might actually have saved his life by relieving the pressure on his heart. Being laid horizontally would have allowed the blood and fluids pooled in his legs to return into circulation, a process assisted by the coolness of the tomb. He might in these circumstances, have regained consciousness and thus seem to be resurrected.' It is somewhat strange that nobody appears to have expected the Resurrection. Even the Apostles were unwilling to believe what they saw after the supposed resurrection, or was it resuscitation? Those who have studied the Roman method of crucifixion affirm that it usually took several days or up to a week for a crucifixion victim to succumb to death, unless the person's legs were broken. The means of death is actually strangulation and asphyxiation. The legs were placed on a block so that the person would be able to support themselves for a long time. The nailing to the cross was psychological more than anything else, as eventually the person became so exhausted that they were unable to lift themselves up any longer, and suffocated. It is extremely unlikely for someone to die by a three-hour crucifixion in the manner described in the Bible. The crucifixion executioners would have had to have been highly incompetent in their job, which is most unlikely. So it is indeed possible that

Christ could have survived the Crucifixion. This is exactly as the Koran and others claim.

Father Günther Schwarz, the German theologian, in his book *Anistemi und Anastasis in den Evangelien*, quoted by Dr Holger Kersten in *Jesus Lived in India*, has proposed an interesting view on the whole question: 'The linguistic evidence is conclusive: not "resurrection" but "resuscitation", is the only meaning possible for both these Aramaic words, one of which Jesus would have used. I am referring to the synonymous words achajuta and techijjuta. Both nouns are derived from the verb chaja "to live", and consequentially mean – I repeat – "resuscitation", and not anything else.'

Hyam Maccaby, in his book *The Christ Myth*, suggests that in the original Greek texts of the gospels, one finds the possibility that the real meaning of the Crucifixion is allegorical. This is because when the Jews asked Pilate to free Bar Abbas they really meant Jesus. When the Greek and Roman translators, unfamiliar with Aramaic or the Messianic implications of the Crucifixion, included the call for release of the convicted, they mistakenly established a separate individual called Bar-Abbas. Of course, without the Crucifixion, there could have been no Resurrection. Many scholars and critics have questioned the possibility of such a remarkable event as the Resurrection, without any precedent in the history of mankind except for the prophet Elijah. For example, the biblical scholar Kirsopp Lake suggests that the women who reported the body missing had in fact probably gone mistakenly to the wrong tomb. Some have suggested that the whole event can be explained by the scientific theory of 'hallucination'. It is also possible that the disciples stole the body from the tomb while the guards were asleep, or that either the Roman or Jewish authorities moved the body from the tomb, which was potentially a source of civil unrest among Christ's supporters. So is the Resurrection a fact or a myth? It raises doubts in the minds of sceptics which are steadily refuted by the believer. The Koran, as we have discussed, dismisses the idea of crucifixion completely.

An interesting book on the whole question of whether or not Jesus actually went to India and Tibet is *The Lost Years* by the American spiritual savant, Elizabeth Clare Prophet, which has been extensively researched by her to provide all sides of the argument. On the perplexing crucifixion question she points out that the orthodox gospel view of the Crucifixion was contradicted by 2nd-century early Church tradition and that Jesus may well have spent many years on Earth after the Resurrection. She quotes that eminent pillar of early Christian orthodoxy, the Church Father Irenaeus who, in his polemic against heresies written circa AD 180, makes the sensational statement that: 'On completing his thirtieth year he suffered, being in fact still a young man, and who had by no means attained to an advanced age. Now, that the first stage of early life embraces 30 years, and that this extends onward to the fortieth year, every one will admit. But from the fortieth and fiftieth a man begins to decline towards old age, which our Lord possessed while He still fulfilled the office of a Teacher, even as the gospel and all the elders testify. Those who were conversant in Asia with John, the disciple of the Lord, affirmed that John conveyed to them that information.' Furthermore, in the 3rd-century Gnostic text the *Pistis Sophia* we read: 'It came to pass, when Jesus had risen from the dead, that he passed eleven years discoursing with his disciples and instructing them.' Consequentially, there is no way of being certain that the four canonical gospels have not been considerably edited by scribes for theological or politic reasons, until they were adopted as the ultimate statements as late as the 4th century AD. The discovery of the Gnostic gospels at Nag Hammadi in 1947 showed that early Christians had a very large and widely different library of over 50 gospels, far more than just the four gospels that were eventually chosen to represent final Church orthodoxy on all questions concerning the life and death of Jesus. So it is not an impossibility that Jesus could have survived the Crucifixion, and that Joseph of Arimathea, knowing full well he was not actually dead, placed him in the tomb. After three days, to fulfil the biblical prophecy, Joseph may have released him from the tomb as he had been resuscitated, and allowed his followers to believe it was resurrection from the dead. Astonishing, impressive miracles, like resurrection from the dead, were absolutely necessary for earnest evangelists like St Paul, to ensure that Christianity would spread like wildfire and become the new world religion, which it did. This escape from crucifixion would have allowed Jesus to then travel to India and Kashmir.

There is, however, an interesting Gnostic text, discovered at Nag Hammadi, which is called The Treatise on the Resurrection. It is an eight-page didactic letter, from father to son, probably written in the late-2nd century AD. It makes the point that belief in the whole question of the Resurrection was really a matter of faith, and cannot ever be proven by rational explanations alone. I shall paraphrase the relevant passage to remove the stilted archaisms. 'But if there is anyone who does not believe, he does not have the capacity or willingness to be convinced. For it is in the domain of Faith, my son, and not in the realm of persuasion and argument, that the dead can arise … for we have known the Son of Man, and we have believed that he rose from among the dead … great are those who believe … What then is the Resurrection? It is always the disclosure of those who have risen. Elijah appeared before Moses, with him do not think that Resurrection is an illusion. It is truth! Indeed it is more appropriate to say that "this world is an illusion", rather than the Resurrection which has come into being through Our Lord, the Saviour, Jesus Christ!'

For the final judgement on this vexed question we must turn to the world-famous Jesus scholar Dr Geza Vermes, who has pioneered work on the Dead Sea Scrolls and the historical figure of Jesus in several masterly books. Oxford professor Vermes, in the final chapter of his book *The Resurrection*, after exhaustive analysis of all the gospel reports and circumstances, states that in his opinion, the reports of the Resurrection and the visions surrounding them satisfactorily convince only the already converted. He thinks we should have been given a uniform and foolproof account to meet the requirements of a scientific enquiry. He lists six theories of explanation of the events surrounding the Resurrection. First, that the body was removed by some person who had no connection with Jesus whatsoever. Second, that the body was removed by his disciples. Third, that the empty tomb was a different one from the tomb of Jesus. Fourth, that buried while still alive, Jesus later left the tomb. Fifth, that Jesus may have left Judaea after being resuscitated. Although Dr Vermes does not entertain this latter theory himself, it would allow the teaching of Islam and the Ahmadiyya sect's propositions to be wholly tenable. Finally, some Christian theologians suggest that Jesus' appearances point to a spiritual or visionary, rather than a bodily resurrection, and that spiritual resurrection lives in the hearts of all Christian men and women, past and present, as a matter of Faith. In the same way, the Christian doctrine of 'Christ in us' acquires so great an importance to the followers of Christianity that the vexed problems of the historical Jesus of Nazareth are quite often relegated to the background.

Chapter 10

Summary and Conclusions

W e are now in a position to carefully review and weigh up all the evidence, in order to come to our own considered judgement, as to whether or not there is in any truth in the claim that Jesus did indeed visit India and Tibet in his 'missing years'. We have read the Aquarian Gospel's Indian and Tibetan chapters, the Gospel of Issa, the Bhavishyat Maha Purana and the Natha Namavali Sutra; we have studied the Islamic point of view and looked at the other possible explanations of how Jesus could have spent his 'missing years'. Let us first look at the Indian and Tibetan chapters of Levi Dowling's Aquarian Gospel.

The Aquarian Gospel

First, there is no doubt that Dr Levi Dowling was a man of impeccable moral integrity in his personal life. His father was a minister in the respected Disciples of Christ sect. From the age of 13 he entered the field of religious public speaking. At 18 he was selected as the pastor of a church congregation, and at 20 was appointed a Chaplain in the United States Army, serving to the end of the Civil War. He was awarded the great honour of giving President Abraham Lincoln's funeral oration to the Union Army at Illinois. He attended the respected North Western Christian University and became a respected publisher of Sunday school literature. He worked for the cause of the Prohibition of Alcohol Movement, and on top of all that, graduated from no less than two medical schools. He was a trusted, competent medical practitioner. He was the author of two well-received spiritual healing books. He taught chemistry, toxicology, physiology, histology and researched the use of electricity in medicine. His fundamental honesty was never questioned during the 67 years of his valuable life dedicated to serving his fellow men.

William C Weston MD, a medical colleague, had this to say about Dowling: 'Levi was a faithful and beloved leader, a heralder of good will, an inspirer of noble example, a great hearted man with a finely attuned spirit, catching inspiration from God. His ideal of service was to scatter sunshine and love into darkened lives, blotting out the unsightly places, and bringing in their stead the lovable and beautiful.'

So there is no suspicion, in any way, that he may have been a self-appointed charlatan. But we have to look closely at the whole validity of spiritual mediumship and channelling, if we are to believe his words can be safely relied upon. The first question we need to ask is what exactly is spiritual channelling and mediumship?

Spiritual channelling is a process whereby a highly gifted individual becomes a channel or conduit for 'the spirit world'. In particular, it requires the power to make sure the mind is absolutely calm and free of any obtrusive thoughts. Most cultures have had inspired channelers in the form of oracles, seers, shamans, prophets, temple priests, diviners and priest-esses throughout the ages, particularly in the ancient civilizations. In a sense it may be called an art rather than a craft. When a spiritual medium uses channelling they are leaving their normal state of waking consciousness and becoming a channel for a source of energy not normally entering the human field of awareness.

Regarding Levi Dowling's qualifications for such a role, we are assured by his second wife Dr Eva Dowling that as a boy, he was fascinated with the idea of the sensitiveness of 'the fine ethers' and believed there were sensitized plates on which sounds and thoughts were impressed. With persistence he made a deep study of 'etheric vibration', and was determined to solve great heavenly mysteries for himself. He spent 40 years of study, fasting and meditation in this quest, until he found himself in that stage of 'spiritual consciousness' that allowed him to enter the realm of these superfine ethers and become familiar with their mysteries.

So we can assume that Dowling was well qualified to attempt this arduous art. What is interesting, and unusual, is that he did not rely on a 'spirit guide' from another plain for his revelations. Instead he went directly to the Akashic Records or 'God's Holy Book of Remembrance'. The word 'akashic' is Sanskrit for 'the primary or primordial substance, sky, space or ether, out of which all things are formed'. It is the first stage of the crystallization of the spirit. This philosophy recognizes that all primordial substance is in fact spirit, and that matter is only spirit moving at a much lower rate of vibration, becoming a coagulum; that is, a change from a fluid to a more or less solid state.

According to those who believe in this theory, the akashic, or primary, substance is of such exquisite, subtle fineness, and is so highly sensitive, that the very slightest vibrations from any point in the universe will register an indelible impression on it. Furthermore, this primal substance is not confined to any particular place in the universe, but is omnipresent. It is another name for the 'Universal Mind', a term used by many academic metaphysicians, or 'the Collective Unconscious', a concept developed by Carl Jung. So, when the mind of an individual is exactly tuned into the Universal Mind, he or she can enter into a conscious recognition of these Akashic Records or impressions. He may then transcribe them into his own language. To many they make clairvoyance and psychic perception possible. They are the library of all events and responses concerning consciousness in all realms, a kind of universal, cosmic morphogenetic field.

Eva Dowling, who was a Doctor of Philosophy, makes the interesting observation that 'In the Infinite One manifest, we note the attributes of Force, Intelligence and Love', It therefore follows that a gifted, trained and experienced medium, with a relatively purified consciousness, may well be in full accord to receive any one of these attributes. But it is from the Universal Mind, which is Supreme Intelligence, that the Akashic Records or the 'Holy Book of God's Remembrance' can be drawn. In higher consciousness studies we note there are three distinct realms: Consciousness of God's Omnipotence, Consciousness of Divine Love, and Consciousness of Supreme Intelligence. The Akashic Records are wholly in the realm of Supreme Intelligence. The channeler or medium must be able to discriminate skilfully enough, to receive, read and transcribe the thoughts and life events of any particular individual or group of individuals on which he focuses, to the degree that every thought vibration is instantly felt in every fibre of his being.

When the channeler fully understands the law of dispassionate, intellectual discrimination, his whole being is then finely tuned for the reception of the desired selected tones or rhythms. This is analogous with very high frequency, digital radio or television reception. In Levi Dowling's case, we are informed by Eva Dowling that it took him very many years of painstaking study to learn and practise the law of differentiation and to find rapport with the tones and rhythms of none other than the Lord Jesus Christ. But under the direction of the Spirit of Supreme Intelligence, he attained this accomplishment, and could instantly feel in all his being the slightest vibration that came from this great centre. Eva Dowling assures us that all his transcriptions are true to the letter.

If one accepts the moral purity, excellence, efficiency, skill and diligent assiduity of Levi Dowling, and the testimony of Eva Dowling, then the discussion is over, and the reader can well accept the Aquarian Gospel as a true record of Jesus' life and his visitation to India and Tibet, although it does somewhat differ in detail from the Tibetan chapters in the Gospel of Issa.

Scholars have found certain discrepancies between his gospel and historical facts. He misidentifies Herod, calling him Herod Antipas, when he was actually Herod the Great. He mentions Jesus visiting Lahore, which did not exist in this period. He claims that Jesus knew Meng-tzu, which is impossible because the Chinese sage predates Jesus by three centuries. These errors are, however excused, on the grounds that to receive every single detail from the voluminous Akashic Records absolutely accurately would need a degree of exceptional, superhuman, fine mental tuning, which could explain an occasional slip.

Levi Dowling's Aquarian Gospel has a very large following in the United States of America. These include the Aquarian Christine Church Universal, The Christian Church (Disciples of Christ), and the Aquarian Gospel Reading Fellowship. The gospel has never been out of print and has influenced many in the worldwide new age movement. Other psychic mediums who also claim to have been able to access the Akashic Records are major figures in the Theosophical Movement such as Madame Blavatsky, Annie Besant and Charles Leadbeater; as well as prominent modern mystics such as Edgar Cayce, Alice Bailey, Manley P Hall, Dion Fortune and Rudolph Steiner.

Author Dr James Ocansey has gone on public record by stating: 'if Christians recognize revelation knowledge as coming from the Holy Spirit, then we must also recognize the revelation given to one Levi, a 19th-century American, who transcribed from the Book of God's Remembrance much detailed information about the Lord Jesus Christ. Outside of the four accepted gospels, there was no way anyone could have known the life of Jesus Christ without having received it directly from the Holy Spirit (Holy Breath). According to him they were transcribed from the "Akashic Records" from which he recorded information to fill in the missing years of Jesus Christ.'

But many readers may feel it is all too far fetched and out of the bounds of human possibility, and that such a state of mind, and the existence of Akashic Records, is not a supportable tenet without independent, impartial scientific enquiry and evidence. They may come to the conclusion that Dowling, deeply sincere as he may have been, was under some delusion, and was really channelling a version of events, original as they are, which sprang from his own subconscious or unconscious mind, and really only echoed his own theological understanding of Jesus' historic mission.

Without labouring this point too much, we must leave it to each reader to decide for himself. However, the Aquarian Gospel is not the only evidence for Jesus' journey to India and Tibet. We have Notovitch's discoveries, and the Islamic point of view, with archaeological evidence to consider, before coming to a personal judgement. So let us now look at the Gospel of Issa.

The Gospel of Issa

Nicolai Notovitch was a Russian Cossack officer, a successful journalist, an Orientalist, explorer, playwright, diplomat and author. Whether these are sufficient qualifications to claim he was a man of complete moral integrity, we have to leave to the reader to decide. There is some suspicion that he may have been a government spy as well, and part of the espionage network employed by the Russian government abroad. This fact, if true, is clouded in obscurity, for obvious security reasons. Even being a suspected spy does not impugn his ethical standards, although it may lead people to think he was a man capable of duplicity, which fuelled any ambition he might have had for money and fame. Strangely, after the publication of his sensational book, *The Unknown Life of Jesus*, he was arrested by the Russian authorities because of literary activity deemed dangerous to the state! Although temporarily exiled to Siberia, he was never tried, so one assumes the case could not be proved. The French, however, did elect him as a member of their celebrated Society of Diplomatic History, which gives some indication that his colleagues believed him to be a gentleman of impeccably honest repute. So again, whether he was a man of truth must be left to the reader's judgement. In fairness to Notovitch, who exhibits no knowledge of Islam and makes no record of his second visit to India and Kashmir in his resumé, Issa is an Islamic name for Jesus, and Moses is called Mossa. So the fact that these names are used in the Tibetan manuscripts possibly points to authenticity, as they are unlikely to have been invented by Notovitch, who was apparently unfamiliar with the Islamic religion.

In addition there is substantial evidence for his discovery by respectable and trusted witnesses, who say that they have also seen the actual Gospel of Issa for themselves. First, there was the venerated Indian Sanyasin, Swami Abhedananda, (Kaliprasad Chandra), a graduate of the Oriental Seminary in Calcutta and an acquaintance of Professor Max Muller, whose name seems to keep on cropping up in this investigation. In 1922, the swami went on a pilgrimage to Tibet. He visited the Hemis Monastery, and enquired as to whether Notovitch's discovery was true. The abbot said that it was true, and according to his testimony, showed him the manuscript, said to be a copy of the original text from the Marbour Monastery at Lhasa. The abbot then helped him to make a translation, which I have not been able to find in any literary source. Whether this was a copy of the actual document in Pali we shall never know, and whether Abhedananda knew Pali is unknown. However, as a devout swami, his truthfulness cannot be questioned, although whether he was deceived by the Tibetans, who wished to maintain the legend, strongly rooted in their folk memory, is open to question.

In 1939 a Swiss nun, the Revd. Mother Elizabeth Caspari, visited the Hemis Monastery while on a pilgrimage to Mount Kailasa in the company of Mrs Clarence Gasque, President of the World Association of Faiths. According to Caspari, the librarian showed them the old manuscripts and said, 'These books tell of your Jesus' stay here.' There were three volumes. Although these ladies were obviously of integrity, it is again questionable as to whether the librarian, who was not the abbot, showed them the actual manuscripts. Again, he might have been anxious to preserve the legend for the sake of the monastery's reputation, and guard them from possible theft. We do not know if the ladies knew any Pali, which is doubtful. Also, this is the first mention of three volumes. It may be that the manuscripts were translated for Notovitch by the then abbot and an interpreter into several volumes. Unfortunately, we shall never know the answer to this question.

Then, according to Dr Holger Kersten, the aristocratic travel author Lady Henrietta Merrick: 'confirmed the existence of the writings in her book *In The World's Attick*, published in 1931. She is purported to write "In Leh in the legend of the Christ who is called 'Issa', and it is said that the monastery at Hemis holds precious documents 1,500 years old which tell of the days that he passed in Leh, where he was joyously received and where he preached."' Coincidently, Leh is mentioned by both Dowling and Notovitch as a place that Jesus visited. I did examine her rare travel book, as fortunately the British Library possesses the only known copy. Lady Merrick did indeed visit Hemis, but I could find no record of her stating that she actually had seen the manuscripts in question or making that statement. Dr Kersten also states that a certain Mrs Harvey describes the Tibetan texts in her book *The Adventures of a Lady in Tartary, Thibet, China and Kashmir*, which appeared in 1853. The British Library again has a copy of this rare book. I went through it very carefully and could find no such record. One can only assume that Dr Kersten reports these books as evidence on somebody else's authority, not having access to the British Library's resources himself, as his research was carried out in Germany, so he had to rely on other writers' trusted words.

However, Dr Kersten decided to travel to Tibet in order to see the precious manuscripts for himself, and then on to Srinagar to visit the alleged burial tomb of Jesus. He left Europe in 1979. He first went to Dharamsala to see the Dalai Llama, and requested a letter of introduction to the abbot of the Hemis Monastery granting him permission to examine the manuscripts appertaining to the Gospel of Issa. The Dalai Lama graciously agreed and gave him a signed letter of introduction as requested.

On arrival at the Hemis Monastery, after settling in to stay as a guest, Kersten was greeted by Nawang-Tsering, the secretary and interpreter for the abbot, Dungsey Rinpoche. The secretary told him that he would be granted an audience with His Holiness. While waiting to see the abbot, Nawang-Tsering informed him that the former abbot, also the head of the Duk pa Kagyu sect of Tibetan Buddhism, was assumed to have been taken prisoner since the invasion of Tibet by the Chinese Army. The Chinese government had prohibited all correspondence with him, and he was reported to be held in an undisclosed labour camp. After 15 years' absence a successor was duly appointed at Hemis. There was an Australian, resident at the monastery, who heard about Kersten's reason for visiting the monastery. The Australian spoke Tibetan fluently and agreed to act as his interpreter, because the new abbot spoke only Tibetan. When he met the abbot he showed him the Dalai Lama's letter, and told him how important it was to see these manuscripts. The abbot then informed him that they had searched for the manuscripts in question, but they could not be found. However, there was an old diary, dating from the 19th century, kept in the Moravian Church Mission in Leh, in which the missionary and Tibetan scholar Dr Karl Marx, had recorded Nicolai Notovitch's stay at the monastery in Hemis. Unfortunately, the diary had 'gone missing' some years before, but Professor Hassnain from Srinigar University had photographic evidence of it. On meeting Professor Hassnain, Kersten was able to see the photograph, thus satisfying himself that Notovitch had actually been to Hemis.

So, the only truly reliable witnesses who saw the documents purporting to be the Gospel of Issa were Swami Abhedananda, Elizabeth Caspari and Mrs Gasque, but there is no evidence that any of them knew any Pali. They had to accept the word of the then abbot, his librarian and their translators, that what they were shown was in fact the gospel in question. It is most unlikely that the monks would deliberately lie to them, but actual 100 per cent evidential proof of their existence is still lacking. However, the abbot who saw Swami Abhedananda did assist him in making a translation, so there must have been some form of document which told the story there at that time. Of course, even if we accept the probability that the gospel did exist, we do not know when it was written, so it could well have been composed at a much later date, to consolidate the folk legend that was very much alive in the Tibetan people's minds.

Folk legends and myths are often based on facts, but this would be deemed insufficient evidence to satisfy a scientific enquiry, so we must leave it to the reader to form his own judgement on the facts as we know them.

Following the sensational publication of Nicolai Notovitch's book in 1894, in French, and its subsequent translation into English, there was the expected ecclesiastical outcry against such a supposition. The distinguished and renowned Dr Max Muller, the German Oxford professor, and editor of the 50-volume *Sacred Books of the East* was asked to investigate. He heard from an unnamed British colonial officer, by letter dated June 29th 1894, that he could find no documentary record of Notovitch's visit. To be fair to Notovitch, it must be stated that Muller was prejudiced in advance against such a discovery, as were the Churches. Muller had been on record in correspondence to a friend stating: 'India is much riper for Christianity than Rome or Greece were at the time of St Paul.' He adds that he would not like to go to India as a missionary because that would make him dependent on the authorities and goes on to write: 'I should like to live for ten years quite quietly and learn the language, try to make friends, and then see whether I was fit to take part in doing something that might help to overthrow the ancient evil of Indian priestcraft and to create an opening for simple Christian education.' Muller subsequently commissioned, in 1895, a certain J Archibald Douglas, a schoolmaster at the Government College, Agra, to visit Ladakh with the implicit aim of exposing Notovitch as a fraud. Initially, Douglas reported that he could find no trace of Notovitch having been to Ladakh, but did acknowledge the confirmation by Dr Marx. He allegedly paid a visit to the Hemis Monastery, and said that the abbot had not met Notovitch, and claims that the abbot said '*sun, sun, sun, manna mi dug!*' which Douglas took to mean lies, lies, lies, nothing but lies. But these words quoted are not Tibetan, nor in any Tibetan dialect nor any Asiatic language. The fact that Douglas did not see the documents does not prove that they did not exist, and in any event, Douglas, whose veracity may also be doubted, was sent with the sole purpose of pouring scorn on Notovitch's discovery, and was hardly a reliable witness.

The most powerful attack on Nicholas Notovitch, however, comes from the resolutely committed Christian, and respected academic scholar, H Louis Fader in his book *The Issa Tale That Will Not Die*, with the ominous subtitle 'Nicholas Notovitch and His Fraudulent Gospel'. In a densely argued book of over 260 pages, Louis Fader rigorously attempts to demolish Notovitch's reputation and veracity, despite admitting, over and over again, that his hypothesis is growing in popularity both in the East and West. He admits that the idea of the unknown Jesus manuscript seems to lie deeply in the unconscious of a public whose appetite for accounts about the 'mysterious East' is insatiable. In my view, the impact of Buddhist and Hindu mysticism, newly revealed to the West in the 19th and 20th centuries, reinforces the notion and the wished-for belief that Jesus must have somehow known about the ancient wisdom of the Buddha and the Brahmins. It somehow unifies the world's higher religions in a more holistic way. But Louis Fader, uncompromisingly, will have none of that. He cites the several Christian scholars who travelled to Leh and failed to find the manuscript. But they were as predisposed to not finding any missing gospel as the Tibetans, Hindus, Orientalists and Moslems were to finding them, so they predictably failed. The

Tibetan authorities may well have resented persistent Christian enquirers keen to destroy their cherished myth, and carefully hid any information they might have, in case it was torn to shreds by the prejudiced pedagogic mind.

Fader does, however, admit that one Christian scholar takes a different point of view on the existence of the Gospel of Issa: the Roman Catholic author and Barrister at Law, Julien A H Louis, a Fellow of the Royal Geographical Society and respected member of the Indian Buddhist Text Society. Louis wrote: 'the Pali manuscript was an attempt to reabsorb into Buddhism some of the earlier converts to Christianity.' Louis Fader also cites Max Muller's emissary, the schoolmaster Douglas, as one who failed to find the manuscript. But we know that both Muller and Douglas were highly prejudiced about the existence of such a revolutionary document in the first place. He also refers to Reverend Dr E Ahmad Shah, a Christian Missionary, later to become a member of the Executive Committee of the United Provinces Christian Council of India, who also failed to find the manuscripts after a meticulous search, as described in his book *Four Years in Tibet*. Professor Dr Fida Hassnain firmly states in one of his many books on this topic, *The Fifth Gospel*, that Ahmad Shah was specially deputed in 1894 by the Christian Mission to refute the findings. Dr Shah, according to Hassnain, admits this intention in his book. Dr Hassnain has suggested that the lamas probably concealed the manuscripts from Christian enquirers out of fear that either the British or Indian Christian Missionary authorities would try to confiscate them.

Louis Fader also mentions two individuals, an unnamed Kashmiri pandit and an educated high-caste Brahmin from

Bengal named Swami Rama who did not doubt for a minute that Jesus had spent a number of years in their homeland. I suppose they illustrate their nation's desire to have Jesus' holy feet tread on their ancient ground. Even Great Britain has been suggested as a possible destination for the same reason, as William Blake proposed. Swami Rama told the American traveller Edwin Schary that 'we in India have ancient records of your great spiritual leader, Jesus of Nazareth coming to India and disappearing into the great Himalayan Mountains.' I suppose he was referring to the Purana and Natha documents.

Louis Fader also attacks Kersten for accepting Lady Merrick's testimony that she saw the gospels. However, I can excuse Kersten's error, on the probability that he did not have access to this rare book in Germany, and must have simply accepted the word of other people he considered trustworthy. Fader is unhappy about Nicholas Roerich's evidence that most of the Tibetan people definitely believed in the legend as factual. He also quotes an expedition by a Hindu sadhu named Hulder, with three distinguished Moravian Christian missionaries and some Ladhaki Tibetans who went in search of the books and, after persistent enquiries, failed to find them. He throws doubt on the venerated Swami Abhenanda's visit to Hemis; a respected witness who claims to have seen the documents and obtained a translation. He does put forward the esteemed sage, the Parahamsa Yogananda of the Self-Realisation Fellowship, as being another probably wishful-thinking Indian. Yogananda posited the belief that Jesus visited India as a way of paying back the three Indian wise men (Rishis) who welcomed him at the Annunciation. Fader also writes an interesting chapter on the cultural conditions in Notovitch's time which could produce such a phenomenon. He is, however, adamant that Notovitch's discovery was an ingenious hoax perpetrated on the Christian world to further his own personal agenda. He does not suggest any solution to the 19 missing years other than the theory that travel for Jesus was unnecessary, as he could learn all he needed to know in Jerusalem.

Robert Aron, in his book *The Hidden Years*, takes a similar point of view in explaining that a study of Judaism in Jerusalem was sufficient training without the need for further travel. He describes the conventional Jewish education of the time, that Jesus might well have received, in order to make his point. However, in fairness to Louis Fader, Aron also raises many doubts about Notovitch's veracity, and for those who wish to arm themselves with arguments against the possibility of the Gospel of Issa's existence, there is plenty of material given in this closely written book, which I have endeavoured to summarize.

Another novel and unique criticism of Notovitch comes from the Indian Swami Devanata, writing in the public domain, who alleges that the Issa Gospel cannot be true, because according to him the Buddhist monastery where Jesus is said to have studied did not exist until the 16th century, and the Srinigar tomb where he is said to be buried is really the tomb of a Mogul ambassador to Egypt who converted to Christianity while on a tour there. The key, he believes, to unravelling this legend is to study the activities of the 10th-century Nestorian Christian missionaries who passed through Kashmir on their way to China and left crosses on rocks and an abundance of children with biblical names in their wake. He believes that the Hindu and Buddhist ideas found in the New Testament books, including the Sermon on the Mount, were picked up by the gospel writers in Alexandria from Indian pundits and monks who were teaching there. Be it as it may, this is the tale that will not go away, and is destined to roll on and on, because, as the swami says, 'it tickles the romantic imagination of Western travellers and quite a few Indians'.

The Historical Problem

We are now in a position to come closer to our own judgement, and those who are still undecided might like to consider the final conclusion of the great and learned Dr Albert Schweitzer, which I am inclined to share, and have placed right at the very end of this book.

Up to now, no orthodox mainstream Christian Church – Protestant or Catholic – has ever endorsed Notovitch's discovery. But this is not surprising as it would supply a revolutionary and rather unwelcome answer to the vexed question of the 'missing years', which the Church and the four Evangelists have conspired to keep a closed secret for over 2,000 years. We will now look at the whole mystery of the 'missing years' and discuss what is plausible, possible and probable, in the various speculations as to how Jesus spent his youth and early manhood, and why the gospels are silent. Before then we must discuss the two Hindu scriptures which claim to be evidence of Jesus' sojourn in India.

The Bhavishyat Maha Purana and the Natha Namavali Sutra

Although the Puranas are greatly revered, and bear all the authority of holy scripture, there are considerable problems in dating them exactly. Along with the Vedas, the Upanishads, and the Bhagavad Gita, they constitute the main body of Hindu religious texts. It is generally accepted that from the 5th or 4th century BC until the 17th century AD they have been constantly extended, with the addition of further narratives, mainly about the mythological activities of the various gods in the Hindu pantheon. The Bhavishyat Maha Purana is believed to have been written sometime between the 3rd and 7th centuries AD, although Dr Hassnain believes it to have been written as early as AD 125. To this extent we may regard its evidence as possibly unreliable, as this addition to the main Puranic corpus, may have been made to substantiate the whole case for Jesus having been actually seen in India, well after the actual date. So again, we are in the realm of supposition, and although we should be able completely to trust the veracity of scriptural authors and scribes, doubts and problems continue to arise. So again the judgement falls on the personal inclination of the reader, as to whether he accepts this whole thesis or not. If he does, then there is no doubt that this Purana is a weighty, authoritative support.

The Natha Namavali Sutra is a scripture held by the mystical order of the Nath Yogis. These Shavite-centred monks belong to one of the oldest Hindu orders, and their origins considerably predate Jesus Christ. Again they must be trusted, and there is no suggestion that they had a vested interest or motive in adding this sutra to their body of texts. Again, if on the weight of evidence so far offered, the reader believes that Jesus was in India, than this is an added scriptural support.

The Islamic Point of View

The Koran is a highly revered and greatly respected scripture. Like the Bible and the Vedas and Buddhist Sutras, it is the key work and the foundation of a great higher religion. It is to Islam as the Bible is to Judaism, the Vedas to Hinduism and the Buddhist sutras are to Buddhism. So it becomes a matter of personal religious faith to accept and believe that the Koran, a scripture revealed to the Prophet Mohammad by the Angel Gabriel, is undeniably true. When the Koran states that Jesus escaped the Crucifixion, adherents to that religion have no doubts whatsoever. Those of other faiths must have recourse to their own traditions, and the historical sources on which they rely. However, there is a considerable body of literature outside of the Islamic tradition which supports this view, and it makes it plausible for Jesus to have travelled to India, a second time after the 'missing years', settled in Kashmir and died there. The whole question of whether Jesus could have escaped the Crucifixion has been discussed separately in chapter 9. As the Islamic point of view is a matter of personal religious faith, and backed up by respected Islamic scholars, it would be wrong to dispute this part of the Koran.

Parallels between Christianity, Hinduism and Buddhism

Because of the strong parallels found between these three higher religions, it has always been a strong part of the case for his presence in India and Tibet that Jesus must have visited these lands to learn about their teachings. However we know, from contemporary historians, that exponents of these faiths had visited ancient Greece, and that this knowledge had also been passed on to Rome, and then could well have been current in Jerusalem, then a part of the Roman Empire. A sceptic may well argue that there is a commonality of religious experience in all the higher religions in any case, not necessarily dependent on the possibility that Jesus could have visited India and Tibet.

The Christian Point of View

All the Christian Churches, except for those American sects that adhere to the validity of the Aquarian Gospel, dismiss the thesis that Jesus went to India completely out of hand, without feeling the need for any real counterargument against a proposition which they regard as outlandish and do not even attempt to disprove. None of them, however, can offer a convincing solution to the problem of the 'missing years'. Therefore the possibility of Notovitch's, Dowling's and Islam's points of view, that he did go to India, Tibet and Kashmir, cannot be totally discounted and considered in any way, an impossibility.

The Missing Years

The Churches have maintained the adamant silence that was kept by the four Evangelists on this whole question. It is obvious, however, that Jesus must have occupied his time somehow in the years before his great mission commenced. He was not just a carpenter. So we are only left with possible conjectures, with no concrete evidence in support of any of them. The official attitude seems to be that he must have stayed in Jerusalem with his family, assisting his father, if needs be, with his craft of carpentry, and furthering his knowledge of the Hebrew scriptures. But it seems most unlikely that such a prodigious and powerful spiritual personality did not occupy himself, one way or another, in more detailed and deeper spiritual study and research, to prepare for his momentous mission on Earth.

So you, my dear reader, must make up your own mind on this vexatious, but nevertheless intriguing question. For those who doubt his journey to India and Tibet, membership of either the Essene or Theraputae communities seems to be the most probable explanation of the 'missing years'. He would have felt completely at home within either order, and would have benefitted from their ascetic way of life, a tendency he later demonstrated to the full, in his great and historic ministry.

The Historical Problem

Perhaps the best authority on this whole question of the historical Jesus is the renowned physician, African explorer, missionary, musician, Christian theologian and humanitarian; the almost legendary Alsatian, Dr Albert Schweitzer. In his highly important, scholarly and seminal work *The Quest of the Historical Jesus*, he comes to a conclusion that I am inclined to share. It seems to answer the question for all, except for those who temperamentally, or for reasons of their religious faith, personal intuition or inclination, wish to wholeheartedly accept or totally reject the Indian and Tibetan hypothesis. For me, it is rather similar to the question: 'Who really wrote the plays of William Shakespeare? Francis Bacon, the Earl of Oxford, a group of Elizabethan playwrights, or that comparatively untutored man from Stratford-upon-Avon?' It does not really matter in the very final analysis. The fact that we have the glorious cycle of plays is sufficient. So the question of authorship, fascinating as it may be, fades into mere hypothesis, interesting mainly to historians, academics and the genuinely curious.

In their remarkable book *The Original Jesus*, a scholarly study detailing the exact links between early Christianity and Buddhism, the authors Holger Kersten and Elmar Gruber make the most pertinent observation that the real, historical Jesus and his concerns are hidden, like a portrait beneath many layers of varnish added to by the weight of 2,000 years of Church history. This is mainly because there is a great problem in delineating with exactitude the life of the 'Historical Jesus'. First, there is the difficulty dating the four gospels, probably chosen from the many available because of their general synoptic agreement concerning the precise history of Jesus' life. St John's Gospel differs from the others, in the sense that it appears to be strongly influenced by Greek thought, with some traces of Gnostic and possibly Buddhist influence. J Edgar Bruns, the biblical historian, was so convinced about the Buddhist influence that he was impelled to devote an entire book to the question, entitled *The Christian Buddhism of St John!* The fact that all the Evangelists ignore the 'missing years' compounds the problem.

How long after the supposed ministry and crucifixion of Jesus were the gospels actually compiled is a crucial question, because if there is a time gap, there may have been distortions, not only from lapses of memory, but deliberate changes brought about by the early Church and Saint Paul's own policy to distance Christ's mission from Orthodox Judaism. The John Ryland Manuscript, the earliest of the more recently discovered papyrus manuscripts, was written in AD 130. So, as far as we can be certain, as literary evidence, the gospels may have been finally compiled after some judicious editing as late as 130 years after Jesus' birth. This is obviously not in any way as conclusive as a contemporary record. However, William Albright, the biblical archaeologist, challenged this view when he wrote in his book *Recent Discoveries in Bible Lands*: 'We can already say emphatically that there is no longer any solid basis for dating any book of the New Testament after about AD 80, two full generations before the date between 130 and 150 given by the more radical New Testament critics of today.' In *Christianity Today*, issue 7, he writes: 'In my opinion, every book of the New Testament was written by a baptized Jew between the forties and the eighties of the 1st century AD, very probably between AD 50 and 75.' So the very best we have, without a papyrus manuscript to back it up, is that the accepted gospel story was composed at least 50 years, and possibly as long as 75 years after Jesus' birth. The material was probably passed down orally until it was actually written down, taking on board hearsay, legend, myth and folk memory. Then the four synoptic gospels of Matthew, Mark, Luke and

John were generally selected by the early Church fathers, always under the powerful influence of St Paul, as the true record of Jesus' life and ministry. All other apostolic accounts, such as the so-called Gnostic gospels, were later dismissed as heretical by influential Church theologians such as Bishop Irenaeus.

Surprisingly, the Gnostic gospels do not tell us anything about the 'missing years' either. They are primarily concerned with eschatological, cosmological and doctrinal questions. They do, however, contain revelations which the early Church suppressed, such as Jesus' active blood-brother James writing a gospel, and Jesus' close relationship with Mary Magdalene. This scholarly scepticism about the gospel details of Jesus' life has led to much speculation, which clouds the whole picture even further. The overall tendency is to make him the revealer of esoteric systems of the highest Gnostic teachings, common to ancient Greece, Egypt, Babylon and, of course, India and Tibet. India and Tibet, because of their romantic and exotic associations, have always appealed to the popular imagination, besides which the earliest religion known to humanity came from the ancient Rishis of India.

In early Greek and Roman secular literature there is, surprisingly, no contemporary record of this extraordinary human being, Jesus Christ, and the miraculous events which took place around him. The earliest reference to him as a historical personage does not occur until around AD 220 when the historian Tacitus, in his Annals XV, refers to him as the founder of the 'superstitious and mischievous Christian community, upon which the tyrant Nero fastened the guilt of the burning of Rome'. He does add that he was executed by Pontius Pilate during the reign of the Emperor Tiberius. So we have had to wait 220 years before a Roman historian even records his name. The Roman Jewish historian Josephus does refer to Jesus in two paragraphs, but scholars have always been sceptical about whether or not they were later interpolations. There are possible, but similarly disputed, brief references to Jesus, in the works of Pliny and Suetonius; but in truth, the only known life of Jesus rests on the reliability of the accounts given in the four synoptic gospels.

The ancient Greeks knew a great deal about Hinduism. Aristotle was the contemporary and tutor of Alexander the Great, and died within a year of him. He conversed with a Jew in Asia, who came from the region of Damascus and belonged to a sect in that country that was derived from the Hindu philosophers. This is recorded by Josephus in his *Against Apion* I:22. His authority was the philosopher Clearchus of Soli who considered the Jews to be of Hindu origin. This may have been an exaggeration but underneath it there is the possibility that a certain sect had such an origin, as the Kashmiris claim. According to Aristotle, Clearchus gave him and his companions more information than they imparted in return. Now as the Buddha had given a missionary charge to his followers, there is no reason why his monks should not have gone to Syria, even before the mission of the Emperor Asoka in the century before Alexander. If they did, an historical question might be solved: that of the origin of the Essenes, who may have influenced Jesus in his 'missing years'. When the Emperor Alexander conquered part of India he left the author Megasthenes as ambassador to the Court of Patna, and ordered him to write a book on the religion of the Hindus. This was a bestseller in Athens, and became the great authority in the West on Hinduism until the Christian era. The Buddhist Emperor Asoka also brought the religion of the Buddha to the notice of the Hellenic kings. So it is very possible that the youthful Jesus may have learned enough about Buddhism and Hinduism in Jerusalem without ever having to travel to India and Tibet.

Then we come to the Acts of the Apostles: where do they stand? Sir William Ramsay, an eminent archaeologist and the author of *The Bearing of Recent Discovery on the Trustworthiness of the New Testament*, was finally prepared, after lengthy research, to accept that this could possibly have been a mid-1st century document. This means that the Acts could have been compiled around the same time as the ecclesiastically adopted canonical gospels, with their unfortunate time lag of at least 50 years, if not more, after the birth of Jesus. We are faced with the difficult fact that all Bible translations are based on the four synoptic gospels that the early Church decided should be the only official record of Jesus' life and ministry. All other accounts were deemed to be heretical. By the 3rd century AD, there were no fewer than 25 different versions of Jesus' death and Resurrection in the apocryphal Gnostic gospels, many of which were attributed to the Apostles. However, the relevant observation has been made by John Dominic Crossan in his book *The Birth of Christianity* that 'some critics gibe that Historical Jesus researchers are simply looking down a deep well and seeing their own reflections from below, and positivism is the delusion that we can see the water without our own face being mirrored in it'.

Perhaps it is safer to approach Christ through the Holy Spirit rather than through history. Similarly, although we know nothing with absolute certainty about the 'missing years', this does not affect the fact that the magnificent universal religion of Christianity has thrived for over 2,000 years, and has been one of the greatest civilizing forces in the history of mankind. Christ's magnificent ministry of love, faith and compassion shines like a great sun, however much it is obscured by the dark and shadowy clouds of disputed historicity, and it can never be dimmed. That 'Great Sun' is best described by the modern Swiss theologian Hans Urs von Balthasar. He conceives Christ to be the revelation of the form of Divinity, as truth, goodness and beauty. The beauty of divine revelation, in his view, comes to perfection in Christ as a central form of God's glory. When beauty, truth and goodness come together, the glory of God is revealed!

Final Conclusion

The Jesus in India legend still refuses to go away. Why? Partly because for Tibetan Buddhists and Kashmiris, it is firmly rooted in their folk memory as a truth. Even if it is a myth, we know that myths are often based on some vital historical fact, no longer available to modern historians, scholars and biblical researchers. For India, it is appealing to believe that Jesus actually came to that land, and it is an idea to be encouraged, if possible. For Islam, the Crucifixion is denied in the Koran, which is their unquestioned authority on all doctrinal matters. For the Ahmadiyya sect and the Kashmiris, who both rely on their own scriptural texts and folk memory, the idea that Jesus came to India, died and was buried there, is a notion to be robustly affirmed. For Christians, except for the proliferating new age sects, the idea is strenuously opposed because it denies the Crucifixion and the Resurrection. They are the main opponents of the legend, and most skilful in the debate relying on highly educated scholastic investigation. For the ordinary man and woman who thinks freely, the idea is also appealing. The Far East has always held a fanciful, romantic attraction for the West. So the legend will continue, reinforced by more films, documentaries, books, novels and new spiritual mediums.

The great Dr Albert Schweitzer comes to the conclusion in his seminal book *The Quest For the Historical Jesus* that Jesus as a concrete historical personality remains a stranger to our time, but his spirit, which lies hidden in his words, is known in simplicity, and its influence is direct. 'Every saying,' according to Dr Schweitzer, 'contains in its own way the whole Jesus, coming to us as One unknown, without a name, as of old. He comes to those men who knew him not. He speaks to us the same words: "Follow thou me!" and sets us the tasks which we have to fulfill for our time. He commands, and to those who obey Him, whether they be wise or simple, He will reveal himself in the toils, the conflicts, the sufferings which they shall have to pass through in His fellowship; and, as an ineffable mystery, they shall learn in their own experience Who He Is.' Need any more be said?

Bibliography

Ahmad of Qadian, Hadhrat Mirza Ghulam, *Jesus in India: Jesus' Escape from Death on the Cross and Journey to India*, Islam International Publishers, 2003

Aron, Robert, *Jesus of Nazareth: The Hidden Years*, William Morrow, 1962

Bock, Janet, *The Jesus Mystery*, Aura Books 1980

Borg, Marcus J, *Jesus and Buddha: The Parallel Sayings*, Ulysses Press, 2004

Carpenter, J Estlin, *Buddhism and Christianity: A Contrast and a Parallel*, Hodder & Stoughton, 1923

Crossan, John Dominic, *The Birth of Christianity: Discovering What Happened in the Years Immediately After the Execution of Jesus*, HarperOne, 1999

Dowling, Reverend Levi H, *The Aquarian Gospel of Jesus the Christ: The Philosophic and Practical Basis of the Religion of the Aquarian Age of the World and of the Church Universal*, DeVorss & Company, 1972

Edmunds, J A, *Buddhist and Christian Gospels, Being Parallels from the Pali Text*, 1904

Faber Kaiser, Andreas, *Jesus Died In Kashmir: Jesus, Moses and the ten lost tribes of Israel*, Gordon & Cremonesi, 1977

Fader, H Louis, *The Issa Tale That Will Not Die: Nicholas Notovitch and His Fraudulent Gospel*, University Press of America, 2003

Hanh, Thich Nhat, *Living Buddha Living Christ*, Rider & Co, 1996

Hassnain, Professor Dr Fida, *A Search For The Historical Jesus: From Apocryphal, Buddhist, Islamic and Sanskrit Sources*, Down-to-Earth Books, 2004

Healey, Kathleen, *Christ as Common Ground: A Study of Christianity and Hinduism*, Duquesne University Press, 1990

Henderson, Alexander, *The Unknown Jesus*

Jacobs, Alan, *The Essential Gnostic Gospels: Including the Gospel of Thomas & the Gospel of Mary*, Watkins, 2006

Jacobs, Alan, *The Gnostic Gospels: Including the Gospel of Thomas & the Gospel of Mary*, Barnes & Noble, 2005

Kersten, Dr Holger, *Jesus Lived in India: His Unknown Life Before and After the Crucifixion*, Penguin Books, 2001

Kersten, Dr Holger, and Elmar Gruber, *The Original Jesus: The Buddhist Sources of Christianity*, Element Books, 1996

Mayberry, Douglas G, *Jesus The Missing Years*, Raven Report & Transcription Service, 2005

McDowell, Josh, *More Than A Carpenter*, Living Books, 1987

Notovitch, Nicolai, *The Unknown Life of Jesus Christ*, Leaves of Healing Publications, 1990

Ocansey, James K, *Jesus Christ The Missing years & The Mysteries*, iUniverse, 2007

Osborne, Arthur, *Buddhism and Christianity in the Light of Hinduism*, Sri Ramanasramam, 1996

Pappas, Constantine, *Jesus' Tomb in India: Debate on His Death and Resurrection*, Jain Publishing Company, 1991

Patton, Richard G, *The Autobiography of Jesus of Nazareth and the Missing Years*, Amron Press, 1997

Philo of Alexandria Vol 9, translated in the Loeb Classical Library Series

Potter, The Reverend Dr Charles Francis, *The Lost Years of Jesus Revealed*, Gold Medal Books/Fawcett Publications Inc; 2nd edition, 1959

Prophet, Elizabeth C, *The Lost Years of Jesus: Documentary Evidence of Jesus' 17-Year Journey to the East*, Summit University Press; 2nd edition 1988

Reynolds, Alfred, *The Hidden Years*, Cambridge International Publishers, 1982

Schonfield, Dr Hugh, *The Passover Plot*, Bantam Books, 1977

Schweitzer, Dr Albert, *Quest of the Historical Jesus: A Critical Study of its Progress from Reimarus to Wrede*, Macmillan, 1968

Scribe, *The Fragments of the Hidden Years of Jesus*, C W Daniel, 1938

Tully, Mark, *Lives of Jesus*, Penguin Books Australia Ltd, 1997

Watson, Hazel, *Unknown Jesus*, Arthur H Stockwell Ltd, 2002

Index